500 Prayers for Young People

500

PRAYERS
FOR YOUNG PEOPLE

Prayers for a new generation

Martin Saunders

MONARCH
BOOKS

Oxford, UK & Grand Rapids, Michigan, USA

First published in the UK in 2011 by Monarch Books
(a publishing imprint of Lion Hudson plc)
Wilkinson House, Jordan Hill Road, Oxford OX2 8DR, England
Tel: +44 (0)1865 302750 Fax: +44 (0)1865 302757
Email: monarch@lionhudson.com
www.lionhudson.com

ISBN 978 0 85721 017 3 (print)
ISBN 978 0 85721 207 8 (epub)
ISBN 978 0 85721 206 1 (Kindle)
ISBN 978 0 85721 208 5 (PDF)

Distributed by:
UK: Marston Book Services, PO Box 269, Abingdon, Oxon, OX14 4YN
USA: Kregel Publications, PO Box 2607, Grand Rapids, Michigan 49501

The text paper used in this book has been made from wood independently certified as having come from sustainable forests.

British Library Cataloguing Data
A catalogue record for this book is available from the British Library.

Printed and bound in the UK by MPG Books Ltd.

Acknowledgments

Huge thanks are due to the greatest magazine staff in the world, Team *Youthwork*, without whom this book would not exist. I'm especially thankful to Laura Haddow, Helen Crawford, and Sean Skinner – all of whom contributed prayers to this book, but each of whom contributed far more to me in encouragement and copious amounts of diet cola.

Contents

Introduction

There's not a lot to do in solitary confinement. All being well, most of us will never see the inside of a cramped, dark cell, where the only entertainment to be found is in counting the footsteps of the guard outside. Yet if, through some strange collision of circumstances, you found yourself in such a place, what would you do?

The answers to that question can form only a very short list. In solitary, you have no resources, no light, and no one to talk to. Well, almost. Because, as many people persecuted around the world for their faith have discovered, the one thing they can't take away from you is prayer.

When everything else is stripped away, prayer is mankind's last resource. Wherever we are, however old we might be, even if we've lost the power of speech, we can still pray.

In the writer Mark Yaconelli's words, "Prayer is home" (in the article "Coming Home", *Youthwork*, May 2008). It is the thing we can return to when everything else has failed us; when we're defeated; when we're lost; when we're broken-hearted. And it's not just something we can do in those times; it's something we're programmed to *want* to do.

When sudden, unexpected circumstances hit, even the most hardened atheist can turn to prayer. When our lives are interrupted by something that shocks and unnerves us, sometimes the frowned-upon reaction "Oh my God" is less blasphemy than it is a simple acknowledgment of truth – a tiny, desperate, automatic prayer.

The desire and need to pray is created inside each one of us at the same time as we get spleens, eyeballs, and collarbones. Like a computer program that is created to contact its manufacturers regularly and "request latest updates", so we are born with an innate desire to talk to our maker.

That's why, in those desperate moments when we do turn to prayer, we instantly feel some degree of comfort. That's why, to stretch the software analogy a little further, we often walk away from prayer feeling refreshed, updated and upgraded.

WELCOME, WHOEVER YOU ARE

"What a lovely present," you may have said but not thought as you were passed what will inevitably have become a "gift book". Or perhaps you glanced at the cover in a bookshop somewhere and, attracted by the "bumper-value" aspect of getting 500 of something, excitedly decided to buy – almost at the same time aware that this will probably end up gathering dust in the wishful-thinking department of your bedroom shelf. Maybe you're neither of these; you could just be someone who wants to inject a bit more prayer into your life, and thought that this sounded like a jolly sensible resource for a person with such an aspiration.

Whoever you are, my aim over the next few pages is to convince you that this collection of prayers isn't best suited for dust-collecting or for your next trip to the local charity shop (yes, I am fully aware of the potential irony here), but deserves a regular and dynamic place in your life. I'm not expecting you to take it out with you on a Friday night, but, in putting it together, I've aimed to create a book that will reward your investment every time you open it. So, as a result, I'm hoping you'll want to keep opening it.

The book contains, as you know by now, 500 prayers that I have considered suitable, useful, relevant or important for people journeying through the alternately marvellous and agonizing teenage years. Which immediately poses an important question: who am I, and what gives me the right to tell you what to pray? I'm a youth worker; I volunteer at a medium-sized (whatever that means) youth group run by my local church, and help to run talks, small-group discussions and activities. I am entirely unremarkable in this regard, and by no means the best youth worker around (although I did win bronze in the fictional 2004 World Youth Worker championships). But I do at least know some teenagers, which I hope gives me the edge over other people who might choose to write such a book, notably politicians. As well as doing this in my "extra" time, my day job is editing *Youthwork* magazine, which is the UK's leading Christian youth-work resource. This is a bit like saying the Thames is London's leading river, because of course there aren't any other major ones. But it sounds good at dinner parties and in book introductions. Plus it gives me some insight into the world that you, the reader, inhabit.

That brings me neatly on to the topic of how this collection has been composed. This is *not* a compilation of prayers written in what I imagine "youth" language to be. As a thirty-three-year-old dad of three, I know the days when I could still have claimed to be young are well behind me. So if you were worried that on these pages you might find such horrors as a prayer written in text-speak, some sort of rap liturgy, or a section called "Da Psalms", you can breathe again. In my experience, teenagers don't enjoy being patronized. Instead, I've brought together prayers from a mixture of sources, which I simply believe you will find relevant and accessible. Some of them are classic prayers, written by saints, martyrs and heroes of the Christian faith; others are reinterpretations of psalms or Bible passages. The majority are original prayers, written by me in straightforward language and in a range of styles. But not including rap. Where I've felt it necessary, I've also included a few words of explanation or application, which you should always feel free to disregard completely. Most of the prayers are written in modern, contemporary English, but one or two I've left untouched in their original, more old-fashioned form. I've done this because I think they're much more amazing without my heavy-handed rewriting, and because I credit you with the intelligence and perseverance to be able to enjoy them as they are.

HOW TO USE THIS BOOK

This book is split into a number of sections, basically in an effort to help you to find the sort of prayers that you might be looking for at a given moment. Most of the prayers are designed to be used in an individual setting (where it's just you and God), but many of them will work in a youth group or church context too. In one sense, then, you can view this as a sort of reference book, which you can pick up whenever you're in need of a specific form of words. Yet I hope that's not the only way you'll find yourself using it.

I don't know what the terms "devotional" and "quiet time" mean to you. Ever since I became a Christian, at fourteen, they have been haunting, guilt-inducing reminders to me that I don't spend nearly enough of my time with – or even thinking about – God. When you've made the decision that he exists, and that the point of existence itself is to know him, that's a bit of an oversight. Yet I think part of the problem with prayer is that we get into a cycle of guilt: we don't do any; we feel ashamed that we don't give God even a fraction of our time when we know he deserves our whole life… and so we push ourselves further away from him because we're suffering from a sort of spiritual embarrassment.

Let's just take a reality check at this point, then: God loves it when we spend time with him. Even just a little bit; even if it's been ages since we last spoke to him. Parents of first-year university students are always fraught with worry when, night after night in that first term, the phone doesn't ring. Their world has shifted dramatically – they no longer know where their beloved sons and daughters are each night – and, as the children get wrapped up in the excitement and intrigue of their new life away from home, the parents left behind become gibbering wrecks. And yet, when that phone call finally comes, that home is filled with joy. There is no anger that the call has taken so long, only delight that it has finally been made.

So it is, on a much larger scale, with God. We should never allow ourselves to get caught up in guilt about how long it's been since we last called; we just need to pick up the phone. All of which is a roundabout way of saying that time with God is something we should aim for every day, and never allow to be overshadowed by the failures of yesterday. One of the ways in which you might want to use this book, then, is to give you some words with which to start off that time. Many people don't find it easy to express how they're feeling when talking to someone face to face; if we're honest, it can sometimes feel even harder when the other person is to some extent invisible. So these prayers, whether they offer words of thanks, apology or request, can help to give language to however you're feeling when you come to pray.

PRAYER AS A DISCIPLINE

I'll pop up now and again throughout the book to introduce each section, but, before I let you loose on the prayers, a word or two about my own "devotional" life. A few years ago, I heard a preacher make a very bold claim at the front of the church I was visiting. He promised that, if I made the commitment to pray every day, my life would look very different one year on. At the time I was sceptical, yet, several years on, I believe those words so passionately that I would comfortably preach them myself. Although not always at the pace and in the manner we might like, God *does* answer our prayers. Although it makes little sense when viewed through our limited understanding of reality, he *does* hear every prayer of every person on the earth. In fact I'd go further – I believe he listens intently.

So this book isn't just a series of poems and chants that you can speak into thin air to make yourself feel better; it's potentially a step towards a radically different life. Because, as that preacher promised me, when you start communicating regularly with God himself, you can't really expect things to stay the same. I've taken that idea to heart in my own life only in the last couple of years. I start every day by reading a couple of passages from the Bible, and then praying, probably far too briefly. Because I'm a writer, and that's how I think, I write down all my prayers (this may be completely wrong for you). I've managed at last to get over the cycle of guilt and the mystique of the "quiet time". I keep it very simple, and my suggestion to you is that you do the same, perhaps using this book to help you get started. Why not – however regularly you manage to do it – choose a chapter from the Old Testament and a chapter from the New, select a few prayers that are relevant to your life right now or to the life you hope to live, and just work through them. That definitely counts as a devotional!

Finally, it's worth noting that the writing of this book was a strange experience, because at times I had a very profound sense that it wasn't just me in the room. I'm not suggesting God wrote this book – it's not *that* good. Yet at times the intensive process of writing many prayers naturally and unexpectedly brought me into the presence of the One they were being written for. It felt as if I'd been unwittingly exposed to a sort of spiritual radiation – a feeling of being very close to God was a side effect I hadn't bargained for.

There's nothing special about most of these prayers – certainly not the ones I wrote. But the act of prayer can be very special indeed, and sends humble little people like you and me into the gravitational pull of the almighty God. Prayer is one of the most powerful resources in the universe, and yet we rarely treat it that way. Allow this book to be your launch pad into a life of prayer, and, just as that preacher promised me, your life may never be the same again.

1

Thanksgiving and praise

As a dad of three small children, I seem to spend half my life reminding them to say thank you. Not because I'm obsessed with turning out children so polite that they could walk straight into the cast of *The Sound of Music,* but because my wife and I want them to appreciate the extraordinary privilege they enjoy growing up in the twenty-first-century West. We're determined that they won't take for granted the food, clothing, shelter, possessions, and freedoms offered by the society they've been born into. So whenever they find themselves in receipt of any of these things, we quickly trot out that familiar question: "What do you say?" "Thank you," they reply, struck by a sudden flash of remembrance. And yet ten minutes later, when another privilege is enjoyed or gift received, the words are lost to them once more. Again, they have to be reminded to show their gratitude. Again we have to prompt them: "What do you say?" My children aren't ungrateful – in fact, largely owing to my wife's influence, they're delightful. But they sometimes forget to say thanks, because their lives are full of pressing distractions – they're busy enjoying life to the max (as far as a pre-schooler can!), and sorting out problems (usually involving toy-sharing).

I think we can all be a bit like that. We're all inherently grateful, deep down, for the things we have; especially the things that matter, which usually can't be bought. Yet we're so distracted by enjoying those good things and dealing with our problems that we forget to be actively thankful. I'm certainly as guilty as anyone in this regard. So this collection of prayers isn't offered as guilt inducement from a parent, but as an encouragement to gratitude from a fellow child. Our God has given us so much, and done so much for us. So, now, *what do we say?*

1. Whatever else, thank you

Whatever else is on my mind, God,
Whatever else I fill my time with,
Whatever else I wrestle with,
Whatever else I ask or say,
Over and above it all,
Thank you,
For everything I have; for everyone I know;
For who you are, and for what you've done for me.

2. Thank you for the breath

Thank you, God, for the breath in my lungs;
For the dreams in my heart;
For the energy that courses through my veins.
Put my passion, my hopes, my whole life
To work for you today.

### 3.	Amazed by scale

Extraordinary creator:
Sculptor of the mountains,
Painter of the universal canvas,
I bow in awe as I think of what you have made.

And yet...

You love me; insignificant little me.
My heart is filled with thankfulness
That the same God who crafted galaxies
Made and knows me too.

### 4.	I cannot understand

God, I cannot get my head around the idea that you
	allowed your only Son to die
So that I could live for ever.
I cannot begin to grasp how you are interested in me –
More than that, love me –
When you are the creator of all time and space
	and matter.

So I'll switch off my puzzled mind for a moment,
	and speak from my heart:
Thank you, God, that you love me so very much.

### 5.	You offer life

You offer me life;
Not just life,
But life to the full.
I'll grasp it gratefully,
With both hands.

6. You loved me first

Thank you that you didn't wait for me to catch up;
Thank you that even when I wasn't interested,
Didn't care,
Didn't want to know,
Laughed at the very suggestion of you,
Buried my head in the sand,
Looked the other way,
Rejected you,
Went in my own direction,
You went ahead and loved me anyway.
Thank you that you loved me first,
Loved me through all that,
And will keep on loving me regardless.

7. I cannot comprehend

Lord Jesus, I cannot get my head around
The torture of the cross;
The relentlessness of the beating,
The cruelty of the nails,
The agony of breathing,
The shame of hanging there.

All I can offer is my grateful thanks,
Knowing that a man embraced pain with his
    arms open
And, in doing so, flung wide the same arms to
    embrace *me*.

8. For the simple things

For the simple things, Lord:
For the comforting smell of earth after rainfall;

For the crisp crunching stomp of boots on snow;
For the brilliant rainbow, scything gloriously through
  the sky;
For the things that don't matter,
But which money can't buy,
Thank you.

9.   Grace and mercy

Your grace offers us a life we do not deserve;
Your mercy spares us from the death we've earned.
You pour out both on us; gifts that overflow.
Thank you for your mercy;
Thank you for your grace.

10.   David's prayer of thanks

The Message, *a paraphrase of the Bible by scholar Eugene Peterson,*
puts the Scriptures into modern language that everyone can
understand. This prayer of David, rewritten by Peterson, sees the great
king overwhelmed with thankfulness for the life that he has been given,
full of praise for the character of God, and asking for protection over
everything he loves.

Who am I, my Master God, and what is my family,
that you have brought me to this place in life? But
that's nothing compared to what's coming, for you've
also spoken of my family far into the future, given
me a glimpse into tomorrow, my Master God! What
can I possibly say in the face of all this? You know
me, Master God, just as I am. You've done all this not
because of who I am but because of who you are – out
of your very heart! – but you've let me in on it.

This is what makes you so great, Master God! There is none like you, no God but you, nothing to compare with what we've heard with our own ears. And who is like your people, like Israel, a nation unique in the earth, whom God set out to redeem for himself (and became most famous for it), performing great and fearsome acts, throwing out nations and their gods left and right as you saved your people from Egypt? You established for yourself a people – your very own Israel! – your people permanently. And you, God, became their God.

So now, great God, this word that you have spoken to me and my family, guarantee it permanently! Do exactly what you've promised! Then your reputation will flourish always as people exclaim, "The God-of-the-Angel-Armies is God over Israel!" And the house of your servant David will remain sure and solid in your watchful presence. For you, God-of-the-Angel-Armies, Israel's God, told me plainly, "I will build you a house." That's how I was able to find the courage to pray this prayer to you.

And now, Master God, being the God you are, speaking sure words as you do, and having just said this wonderful thing to me, please, just one more thing: Bless my family; keep your eye on them always. You've already as much as said that you would, Master God! Oh, may your blessing be on my family permanently!

The Message (paraphrase of 2 Samuel 7:19)

11. Hebrew prayer of thanks

This Jewish prayer of thanks is an amazing piece of poetry – a recognition of the awesomeness of God and what he has done for us, and of just how small we are in comparison. As the final lines say, our feeble praise is like a drop in the ocean of what he deserves. And yet our words mean so much to him.

> Though our mouths were full of song as the sea,
> And our tongues of exultation as the multitude of
>   its waves,
> And our lips of praise as the wide-extended
>   firmament;
> Though our eyes shone with light like the sun and
>   the moon,
> And our hands were spread forth like the eagles
>   of heaven,
> And our feet were swift as hinds,
> We should still be unable to thank thee and bless
>   thy name,
> O Lord our God and God of our fathers,
> For one thousandth or one ten thousandth part of the
>   bounties which thou hast bestowed upon our fathers
>   and upon us.

Hebrew prayer

12. For family

> Thank you, God, for my family.
> For the mother who bore me,
> For the father who sparked my creation.
>
> Thank you, God, for my brothers and sisters,
> In my household and in you;

For every brother and sister I have in Christ,
Near to me and far,
I give you thanks.

Give me the strength to honour my parents,
The grace to see my brothers as you see them,
And the wisdom to love them as you have loved me.

13. For friends

Lord God, thank you for my friends. For people to laugh with, to cry with, and to share life with. Thank you for the people they are and the way you have made them. Thank you for everything I love about them, and everything I find difficult about them. Please give them the grace to be patient with me, and help me to be every day a better friend than I was yesterday.

Amen.

14. Thank You, amazing God

Thank you, amazing God.
For your love that reaches us wherever we are
  – thank you;
For not giving up on us, even when we have given up
  on you – thank you;
For sending your Son to walk among us;
Though he was beaten, tortured and killed;
For sacrificing him in order to rescue us – thank you.
We struggle for a word that says it better,
Yet there are no words that can sum up who you are
  and what you've done for us.
So we simply say: thank you.

15. Thank you for the Bible

Thank you for the Living Book;
May your Spirit reach out of every page,
Grab me by the scruff of my neck,
And pull me closer to you.

16. You hear me

Thank you, God, that when I pray,
Say these words out into thin air or broadcast them
    through my heart,
I speak not into cold, silent, indifferent nothingness,
But into the ear of the one true God.

Thank you, God, that you are listening now –
How crazy it seems that you could possibly be
    interested.
Yet you are. And not only that…

Thank you, God, that you don't just hear us but are
    compelled to respond;
That you don't just watch, but act;
That when we cry out, you intervene.
How mind-bendingly incredible it is that the God of
    the whole universe
Hears me.

17. Legendary God

You are truly great, Lord; your name is legendary
    throughout the earth.
Babies and children know it; even the stars and the
    planets scream out your praise.
How is it possible that you're interested in us?

You work on a grand scale and yet you know us
   as individuals.
More than that – you have made us what we are;
You have given us a whole world to look after.
How extraordinary you are!

Based on Psalm 8

18. A Hebrew blessing

Blessed are You, O Lord our God, Eternal King,
Who feeds the whole world with Your goodness,
With grace, with loving-kindness, and with tender
   mercy.
You give food to all flesh,
For Your loving-kindness endures for ever.
Through Your great goodness, food has never
   failed us.
O may it not fail us for ever, for Your name's sake,
Since You nourish and sustain all living things,
And do good to all,
And provide food for all Your creatures
Whom You have created.
Blessed are You, O Lord, who gives food to all.

Old Jewish prayer

19. Thanks that I can say thanks

Thank you, God, for the breath that swells my lungs,
For the synapses that fire in my mind,
For the syllables that roll around my mouth,
And the joy that blazes in my heart
That allows me to say: Thank you.

20. You forgive

You forgive, Lord, the worst wrongs and the most
     despised ills;
Your love punctures blame; it slays the burden of guilt.
I will praise you because your forgiveness covers
     even me,
Wipes even my slate clean.
Whatever I have done, you forgive.
When I put myself in your place I can't understand it,
But I thank you that it's true.
I receive your forgiveness with thanksgiving.

21. The Canticle of the Creatures

*Some of the words of this prayer by St Francis might seem strange –
especially the bit about "Brother Wind" and "Sister Moon" – but, if
you can get past the language, this is a great song of praise that helps
us to give thanks for some of the things in our world that we might
often take for granted.*

Most High, all-powerful, all-good Lord,
All praise is Yours, all glory, honour and blessings.
To you alone, Most High, do they belong;
No mortal lips are worthy to pronounce Your name.

We praise You, Lord, for all Your creatures,
Especially for Brother Sun,
Who is the day through whom You give us light.
And he is beautiful and radiant with great splendour,
Of You Most High, he bears Your likeness.

We praise You, Lord, for Sister Moon and the stars,
In the heavens You have made them bright, precious
     and fair.

We praise You, Lord, for Brothers Wind and Air,
Fair and stormy, all weather's moods,
By which You cherish all that You have made.

We praise You, Lord, for Sister Water,
So useful, humble, precious and pure.

We praise You, Lord, for Brother Fire,
Through whom You light the night.
He is beautiful, playful, robust, and strong.

We praise You, Lord, for Sister Earth,
Who sustains us
With her fruits, coloured flowers, and herbs.

We praise You, Lord, for those who pardon,
For love of You bear sickness and trial.
Blessed are those who endure in peace,
By You Most High, they will be crowned.

We praise You, Lord, for Sister Death,
From whom no one living can escape.
Woe to those who die in their sins!
Blessed are those that she finds doing Your will.
No second death can do them harm.

We praise and bless You, Lord, and give You thanks,
And serve You in all humility.

St Francis of Assisi

22.   The whole earth sing

The whole earth sing with joy
To the Lord God.
All of us, serve him and sing his praise,
With great wide smiles on our faces.

Because we can know God, God who made us
   by hand –
We are his precious possession, his chosen people.
Praise God – he is beyond incredible;
What he says today is true for a million years.

Based on Psalm 100

23. You let me choose

You could have made it so boring.
Our lives could run on rails, but you didn't build
   robots;
You breathed life into man and then let him choose,
   every day, how to live.

And so we carry on, making mistakes, messing up,
   making the wrong decision.
But you don't lose your nerve; you don't give up
   on us.
You keep on letting us choose.

So today I choose to follow you;
I choose to put your ways ahead of mine.
I choose to thank you for making me unique, and for
   giving me free will;

I choose you.

24. A Ghanaian prayer

This extraordinary African prayer contains a few references that might be a little alien to Western eyes, but the passion is infectious and unmistakable. Best read aloud!

> O Lord, O God,
> creator of our land, our earth, the trees,
> the animals and humans, all is for your honour.
> The drums beat it out, and people sing about it,
> and they dance with noisy joy that you are the Lord.
> You also have pulled the other continents out of
>   the sea.
> What a wonderful world you have made out of the
>   wet mud,
> and what beautiful men and women!
> We thank you for the beauty of this earth.
> The grace of your creation is like a cool day between
>   rainy seasons.
> We drink in your creation with our eyes.
> We listen to the birds' jubilee with our ears.
> How strong and good and sure your earth smells, and
>   everything that grows there.
> The sky above us is like a warm, soft Kente cloth,
>   because you are behind it,
> else it would be cold and rough and uncomfortable.
> We drink in your creation and cannot get enough of it.
> But in doing this we forget the evil we have done.
> Lord, we call you, we beg you:
> tear us away from our sins and our death.
> This wonderful world fades away.
> And one day our eyes snap shut, and all is over and
>   dead that is not from you.

We are still slaves of the demons and the fetishes of
   this earth
when we are not saved by you.
Bless us.
Bless our land and people.
Bless our forests with mahogany, wawa, and cacao.
Bless our fields with cassava and peanuts.
Bless the waters that flow through our land.
Fill them with fish and drive great schools of fish to
   our sea coast,
so that the fishermen in their unsteady boats do not
   need to go out too far.
Be with us youth in our countries, and in all Africa,
   and in the whole world.
Prepare us for the service that we should render.

Traditional Ghanaian prayer

25. You draw near

God, we praise you,
For you are holy,
And yet while we are breaking your heart,
You draw near to us.

Sorry

Apologizing to another person can be tricky enough. The old song says that "Sorry seems to be the hardest word", but at least when you can look someone in the eye and you know you've done them wrong, words do usually appear that begin to put the situation right. Apologizing to God can be another thing altogether. For a start, he's invisible, and then sometimes, if we're honest, it feels a bit odd to be apologizing to someone quite so gigantic and important. In the same way that we sometimes wonder how he can possibly have time to be interested in the tiny things we ask him for, it's also pretty strange to us that he should be offended by our relatively small mistakes. Of course they're not relatively small to us, but, relative to the cosmos he created, they seem inconsequential.

Yet the incredible truth is that not only is God interested in our lives and in the things we wish he would do to change them, he's also affected by the things we do wrong. They are two sides of the same coin. Knowing that, we know also that we need to be right with him. Just as it is never good to do wrong to our human parents and then go on living as if nothing has happened, we need to keep coming back to him to say: "God, I messed up; I'm sorry." This next collection of prayers gives some simple words to that need.

26. Your glory; my shame

Lord, when you passed by in front of Moses,
Your glory was so great that he could not see you
   and live;
He had to hide his face from you.
Lord, with all the sin and shame of my life,
How can I not be burned up by your presence?
Yet you forgive; you wipe the slate clean;
You make me right with you and embrace me.
How incredible that the God of glory draws near
   to me,
And yet I will not perish.

27. Lead me not into temptation

Lead me not into temptation, God;
Send me speeding in the other direction.
Forgive me for the mistakes I make on repeat;
Like a stuck record, I can't seem to move on.
Help me to break the cycle, Lord God;
Lead me into a better way of being.

28. Recreate my heart

Recreate, clean up and renew my heart, God;
Though I have sinned, please don't turn away
   from me.
Fill me with your presence; infect me with your joy;

Burn up everything wrong in me with the fire of
   your Spirit.

As you do so,
Give me the words to help others;
The wisdom to lead my friends towards you.
Forgive my sins, and allow me to feel the warmth of
   your forgiveness.

Based on Psalm 51

29. Take my sin away

Take my sin away,
And fill its place with love.

Take selfishness, anger and lust,
And build up in me gentleness and peace.

Take everything I do,
And use it for your glory.

Take from me all darkness,
And illuminate my life.

30. An apology

Dear God,

For the things I do that hurt you, hurt others, and
end up hurting me too, I'm sorry. For the ways in
which I turn away and rebel, I just want to say that
I wish I was different sometimes. For the things I've
done wrong in the past, for everything that's wrong
with the way I live now, and for all the things I'm
yet to do wrong, I'm sorry… God, I feel like such a
failure sometimes.

Please help me to change. Please help me to replace my wrong ways with right ones. Take me and mould me into the image of your Son. Let me know and understand what forgiveness means. I don't want to live in darkness; I want to live in light. Please hear me, God.

Yours, very sincerely,

Me

31. Remind us of your forgiveness

One of Søren Kierkegaard's many amazing prayers, this one helps us to focus not on the weight of our sin, but on the power of our forgiveness in Christ.

Father in Heaven!
Hold not our sins up against us
But hold us up against our sins
So that the thought of You when it wakens in our soul,
    and each time it wakens,
Should not remind us of what we have committed
But of what You did forgive;
Not of how we went astray but of how You did
    save us!

Søren Kierkegaard (1813–55)

32. Drowning in guilt

Hopefully this prayer isn't usually relevant. For those times, however, when we feel totally overwhelmed with guilt about one thing or a whole build-up of stuff, this prayer is meant as a release valve and a reminder that, as the old hymn says, "the vilest offender who truly believes, that moment from Jesus a pardon receives" (from "To God be the Glory" by F. J. Crosby.

God, I'm drowning in guilt.
It's like a fog has descended:
I can't see past the things I've done.
My words stick in my throat;
I feel hopeless, worthless, irredeemable.

You are my only hope, Lord God.
You are the only one with the power –
To forgive sins,
To fill me with hope.
Give me back my worth;
Bring redemption to my story.

In your amazing power, God, I humbly ask:
Pull me out of the depths,
And set my feet on firm foundations.
Forgive me, Lord.
Without you I am lost;
With you I am made new.

33. Mercifully set me ablaze

O Lord,
You have mercy on all;
Take away from me my sins,
And mercifully set me ablaze
With the fire of your Holy Spirit.
Take away from me the heart of stone,
And give me a human heart,
A heart to love and adore you,
A heart to delight in you,
To follow and enjoy you.

Amen.

Anon.

34. Simply sorry

I have no clever words,
Just a heart that is truly sorry.
Forgive me, God, for my sins,
And make me right with you.

35. Ashamed > Forgiven > Renewed

This prayer uses a traditional format, where at the end of each section
we are helped to remember both that God is merciful and that he is an
active listener.

I am almost too ashamed to speak
Because of the things I have done that I know are
   not right.
My guilt curdles in my stomach; I feel sick;
My heart's desire is that somehow I might be put
   right again.
Lord, in your mercy, hear my prayer.

I know in my head that you forgive;
Help me to know the truth of your forgiveness deep in
   my soul.
Take from me the jabbing discomfort of the things I
   have done wrong;
Recharge me with your Spirit; melt my sense of
   condemnation.
Lord, in your mercy, hear my prayer.

Renew me, God, heart, mind and soul;
Create in me a clean heart; turn me away from wrong.
Lead me away from temptation – from making the
   same mistakes.
Make me better; make me more like your Son.

Lord, in your mercy, hear my prayer.

Merciful Father, accept these prayers for the sake of
  your Son, my Saviour, Jesus Christ.

36. Pierce this cold heart

Since in my ingratitude and blindness
to your holy inspirations
I have so often offended you by my sins,
with tears in my eyes
I beg your pardon a thousand times,
and am more sorry for having offended you,
The Sovereign God, than for any other evil.

I offer you this most cold heart of mine,
and I pray you would pierce it with a ray of your light,
and ignite it with a spark of your fire,
which shall melt the hard ice of my sinful soul.

Based on a prayer by Alphonsus Liguori (1696–1787)

37. Once again

Once again, I find myself saying
I'm sorry.
Just like the last time,
I'm sorry.
Even though I know I'll be here again,
I'm sorry.
Knowing you forgive, but not taking that for granted,
I'm sorry.

38. Don't remember

Don't remember my sins, Lord;
Please forget the mistakes in my past.
Blot out the memory of my rebellion from you;
Since you are completely good,
See my imperfection only through the filter of
    your love.

Based on Psalm 25

39. I have not loved you

Merciful God, my maker and my judge,
I have sinned against you in thought, word and deed,
    and in what I have failed to do.
I have not loved you with my whole heart;
I have not loved my neighbours as myself.
I repent and am sorry for all my sins.
God, in your power, forgive me.

Traditional Anglican prayer

40. Confession time

I confess…
That I don't think sometimes;
That I put myself first, most times;
That I forget you for far too much of my time;
That I make mistakes, all the time.
Every hour of my life seems to bring more error;
Reset the clock on my sin, Lord,
One more time.

41. Daniel's prayer of repentance

This paraphrase of a prayer of Daniel is totally applicable to us, even though the prayer was written thousands of years ago. Like Daniel, we worship a God who is perfect; if he couldn't bear to look at us, we'd understand. Yet, just like Daniel, we have access to this God who chooses to forgive everything we do wrong.

Great, awe-inspiring God,
You do not change – your love for us goes on and on.
We have sinned, turned away from you;
Our ways have been wicked.

Lord God, you are so perfect and holy;
When we compare ourselves with you our shame
   paralyses us.
Yet even though we rebel against you,
You, God, are full of mercy, forgiveness and
   compassion.

Now, mighty God, who delivered a nation of millions
From slavery in Egypt, and still performs
   miracles today,
Perform a miracle in me today:
Forgive me; turn your anger from me.

I ask this not because I am worthy,
But because you are made of mercy.
Since I bear your name,
Restore me for a moment to a clearer image of you.

Based on Daniel 9

42. My God

My God, I have nothing to offer that you could
possibly need.
All I have are simple words: sorry, thank you.
And somehow that's enough for you.

43. Confession of selfishness

Father God,
Forgive me my selfishness.
You know:
I have chosen blindness when my eyes had been
opened;
I have chosen to hoard when I could have shared;
To hold on, when I should have passed on.
I have spoken noble words, while my hands and feet
have stayed silent;
Talked of good news, without *being* good news.
I have limited my dreams to the accumulation of stuff;
I have made my own pleasure my main ambition.
Don't stop at forgiveness, God;
Turn my heart upside down and my ways inside out;
Teach me to love as you love,
To see others as you see them.
Start a revolution in me,
That I might learn to put myself last.

44. Make me wholly yours

My Lord and my God,
remove far from me
whatever keeps me from you.
My Lord and my God,

confer upon me
whatever enables me to reach you.
My Lord and my God,
free me from self
and make me wholly yours.

St Nicholas of Flüe (1417–87)

45. Depth of mercy

This hymn was written in 1740, which explains why some of the
language is a bit ancient. It rewards meditation – I suggest reading it
slowly, several times over – and like so many hymns it is packed with
incredible truth about God. The first line reminds us that so often we
take God for granted, when the fact is that he has gone to extraordinary
lengths to bring us close to him. The final verse is Wesley's powerful
opportunity for our response: a chance for us to say, in the light of all
that Christ has done for us, that we are sorry for the things we have
done wrong.

Depth of mercy! Can there be
mercy still reserved for me?
Can my God his wrath forbear,
me, the chief of sinners, spare?

I have long withstood his grace,
long provoked him to his face,
would not hearken to his calls,
grieved him by a thousand falls.

I my Master have denied,
I afresh have crucified,
oft profaned his hallowed name,
put him to an open shame.

There for me the Saviour stands,
shows his wounds and spreads his hands.
God is love! I know, I feel;
Jesus weeps and loves me still.

Now incline me to repent,
let me now my sins lament,
now my foul revolt deplore,
weep, believe, and sin no more.

Charles Wesley (1707–88)

46.   Take this feeling

Take this feeling, Lord,
Of guilt, sorrow, and brokenness;
Take it as a prayer for your forgiveness.
And take this feeling away from me.

47.   To the other end of the universe

Praise God, my heart and soul;
He forgives me all my wrongs and,
Whenever my life goes into decline,
He is there to reverse the descent.
Made of love,
He is bursting at the seams with grace.
Anger does not come easily to him;
He doesn't repay our sins as we deserve.
Instead, he is like the best father imaginable;
Looking on his children with pure compassion.
He has hurled our evil away from us,
To the other end of the universe.

Praise God, my heart and soul;
His kingdom of love will never come to an end.

Based on Psalm 103

48. You know me better

A classic, anonymous prayer that helps us to pray intimately, as we acknowledge that no one knows us better than God; that, in fact, he knows us better even than we know ourselves.

I thank you, Lord,
For knowing me better than I know myself,
And for letting me know myself
Better than others know me.
Make me, I pray you,
Better than they suppose,
And forgive me for what they do not know.

Anon.

49. Your forgiveness brings life

Your forgiveness brings life, Lord God;
Your pardon brings joy.
Because you have taken guilt and condemnation far
   away from me,
I am truly free;
I am truly alive.

50. A cry from a fallen place

Please listen to my cry, Lord,
As I call to you from a fallen place.
I know that if you kept a list of my sins,

I wouldn't have an answer.
But you don't – instead, you forgive.
Not only that; you invite us to turn our lives around;
Follow you; serve you.
I await your orders, Lord God;
Lift me up from this place,
And put me to work for you.

Based on Psalm 130

Growing
with God

Following God isn't just a matter of a one-time decision. There's usually a specific moment at which we decide to do it, but after that the process of following or "discipleship" takes the rest of our lives. I didn't get that at first. I remember where I was when, at fourteen, I made the decision to become a Christian. I was at the church-hall youth group I'd joined a few months earlier when, apparently prompted by a particularly violent game of dodgeball (because there hadn't been any "spiritual" input that evening), I asked one of my youth leaders if I could pray with him. This was something of a surprise to him, since up to that moment I had been about as interested in Jesus as I was in TV decorating programmes. We went into the sanctuary of the church and prayed a simple prayer together. I still remember very clearly the sensation of a joyous rush of energy through my body, as if I had been gently electrocuted by a children's toy. Yet, if I'm honest, the story gets very dull at that point. I should have been inspired by my decision, and by this divine encounter, to go on to develop a close, regular relationship with a God I was now certain existed. But I didn't. For the next eight or so years, I barely maintained contact. I went to lots of churchy activities of course – summer camps, big music events and the like – but I didn't grow as a Christian. Which is to say: I didn't read very much of the Bible, I didn't do a lot of praying, and my life didn't look very different from anyone else's. I had friends who had no interest at all in faith, and who lived far more kindly, generously, and honestly than I did. I rectified things in my early twenties, but you might quite fairly be thinking: what right does he have to tell me to pray when *he* didn't? All I can say is that I know from experience the benefits of *not* growing in your faith. There are none. At fourteen I had the opportunity to launch myself into an adventure with the creator of the universe – who has the power to do anything I ask or imagine, and more besides. Instead, I chose not to do so for almost ten years. It's a big regret, and my hope is that this book might help you to avoid doing the same.

This next collection of prayers, then, is designed to help us as we seek to grow in our faith. Many of them were written by men and women who knew what it means to throw your whole life into the journey towards God. As you pray through them (these are particularly suited to use in a regular devotional time), I hope you'll be drawn closer to the God who is devastatingly real, and who does not deserve to be ignored.

51. Prayer of St Francis

This prayer is attributed to St Francis of Assisi, who lived in the thirteenth century, although no early copies of it now exist. The language is a bit old-fashioned in places, but I've included it because it's

such an amazing mission statement for any Christian to sign up to. By
praying this prayer, we're asking God to help us to be a force for good in
the world – in our homes, schools and communities.

> Lord, make me an instrument of your peace.
> Where there is hatred, let me sow love.
> Where there is injury, pardon.
> Where there is doubt, faith.
> Where there is despair, hope.
> Where there is darkness, light.
> Where there is sadness, joy.
>
> O Divine Master,
> Grant that I may not so much seek to be consoled, as
>   to console;
> To be understood, as to understand;
> To be loved, as to love.
> For it is in giving that we receive.
> It is in pardoning that we are pardoned,
> And it is in dying that we are born to eternal life.
>
> Amen.

52. Interrupt my day

> Interrupt my day, God –
> Bring people into my line of vision who need my help;
> Bring to my attention where you are at work;
> Bring me to a standstill.
>
> Stop me in the street, God –
> Let nothing be more important than your agenda;
> Let me hear the crackle of your Spirit moving like
>   electricity;
> Let me be a conductor of your power in the world.

53. Give me your peace

I know that over time
Things will happen in my life
That will confuse me,
Make me feel small and out of control
And cause me pain and sadness.

But I thank you for the peace that you've placed in
    my heart
Which reassures me that you are with me even
    through the most difficult of times;
That in every storm that comes my way you are there
    with me, at my side.

Father, as I pray that you will help me to grow in all
    areas of my walk with you,
In my faith and my character,
I also pray that you will teach me to feel and
    understand your peace more and more,
To remember that it is not dependent on my emotions
    and how I feel
But that your love for me never changes,
That I am always on your mind,
And that nothing can separate me from you.

Laura Haddow

54. Wish list for spiritual growth

*This prayer, incredibly written around 1,500 years ago, can act like a
wish list for the sort of character we might hope to have.*

Gracious and holy Father,
please give me:
intellect to understand you;

reason to discern you;
diligence to seek you;
wisdom to find you;
a spirit to know you;
a heart to meditate upon you;
ears to hear you;
eyes to see you;
a tongue to proclaim you;
a way of life pleasing to you;
patience to wait for you;
and perseverance to look for you.

Grant me:
a perfect end,
your holy presence.
A blessed resurrection,
And life everlasting.

St Benedict (480–547)

55. Help me to make time

As I allow myself to believe that I'm too busy to pray,
Help me to realize that I'm too busy *not* to.

As the world around me tells me it's just a book,
Open my eyes to your living word.

As I let myself be sidetracked, distracted,
Bring me back to your presence again, God.

56.   Lead me

Lead me, God, in the pursuit of you;
Change and mould me so that I might be without
   blame,

A speaker of truth, who won't turn on his friends;
Generous almost to a fault, and slow to pursue debts;
A keeper of promises, even when it hurts.
Lead me on this path, Lord, however narrow;
Bring these things about in me.

Based on Psalm 15

57. Fill me

*This prayer directly asks God to fill us with his Holy Spirit. It is
deliberately conversational and chatty because, as Christians, we can
know supernatural things as a natural part of our lives.*

Whatever it means to be filled with your Holy Spirit,
I ask you to do it. If the power displayed at Pentecost
is available to me today, then I want to plug into it. I
want to know you, God, in every way that's possible;
I want to serve you and I know I need to change to
do it properly. Pour your Spirit into me, then, like an
ice-cold glass of water. Through your supernatural
presence in this room, right now, I pray you would
begin to transform me.

Amen.

58. Prayer for wisdom and understanding

Give to me, O Lord my God,
An understanding that knows you,
Wisdom in finding you,
A way of life that is pleasing to you,
Perseverance that faithfully waits for you,
And confidence that I shall embrace you at the last.

St Thomas Aquinas (1225–74)

59. Growing in love

Lord, I want to be known for love;
I follow a God who is made of it.
Enlarge my heart, and let me see others through
   your eyes;
Put my hands to work and purify my words,
That I might be known for love.

60. Night-time prayer

Be with me, merciful God, and protect me through the
silent hours of this night, so that I, tired and weary at
the hands of this ever-changing world, might rest in
your eternal changelessness.

Based on a prayer from the Leonine Sacramentary

(fourth century)

61. A firm place to stand

God, as I patiently wait on you, I know that you hear
   my cry.
You lift me out of dark places when I wander into
   them;
You give me a firm place to stand, which is on you.
Like a dad, hoisting a child onto his shoulders,
You take me out of harm's reach.
You have put words of praise into my mouth:
I feel like singing.

Based on Psalm 40

62. Don't forget

O Lord,
you know how busy I must be this day.
If I forget you,
do not forget me.

Sir Jacob Astley (before the Battle of Edgehill, 1642)

63. For the companionship of Christ

O blessed Jesus, who drew near to your disciples,
so draw near to us as we journey along our daily way.
Open to us the meaning of life,
and reveal yourself as our strength and our
    companion;
You are our Lord and Saviour for ever.

Amen.

Based on a traditional Anglican prayer

64. You light a path for me

God, you light a path for me through life;
Your promises are good both now and into eternity.
I know that because I am your child I am protected,
That anyone who rises up against me will fail.
If a man stands against me, if even a whole army
    does so,
I know that you are on my side and that is always
    enough.
So the only thing I ask is to stay this way for ever –
I know that you will never let go of me.
For my part, I will hold on tightly to you too.

And not only do I look forward to the day we meet
    face to face,
But I am also hungry to see your kingdom come
    here, now.
I want to see your goodness break out here on earth.
Please let that happen, in my life, in my community –
Lord, I wait expectantly for it.

Based on Psalm 27

65. St Patrick's Breastplate

This prayer, written by St Patrick in the ninth century, is the prayer equivalent of a caffeine-packed energy drink, or a sportsperson's pre-match psych-up routine. It's a powerful reminder that we find ourselves in a spiritual battle; that we're part of a story that stretches back through generations and thousands of years; that God is huge, and that following Jesus is an adventure beyond any other. It's also my favourite prayer in this entire book.

I arise today
Through a mighty strength, the invocation of the
    Trinity,
Through belief in the threeness,
Through confession of the oneness,
Of the Creator of Creation.

I arise today
Through the strength of Christ's birth with his
    baptism,
Through the strength of his crucifixion with his burial,
Through the strength of his resurrection with his
    ascension,
Through the strength of his descent for the judgment
    of Doom.

I arise today
Through the strength of the love of Cherubim,
In obedience of angels,
In the service of archangels,
In hope of resurrection to meet with reward,
In prayers of patriarchs,
In predictions of prophets,
In preaching of apostles,
In faith of confessors,
In innocence of holy virgins,
In deeds of righteous men.

I arise today
Through the strength of heaven:
Light of sun,
Radiance of moon,
Splendour of fire,
Speed of lightning,
Swiftness of wind,
Depth of sea,
Stability of earth,
Firmness of rock.

I arise today
Through God's strength to pilot me:
God's might to uphold me,
God's wisdom to guide me,
God's eye to look before me,
God's ear to hear me,
God's word to speak for me,
God's hand to guard me,
God's way to lie before me,
God's shield to protect me,
God's host to save me

From snares of devils,
From temptations of vices,
From everyone who shall wish me ill,
Afar and anear,
Alone and in multitude.

I summon today all these powers between me and
  those evils,
Against every cruel merciless power that may oppose
  my body and soul,
Against incantations of false prophets,
Against black laws of pagandom,
Against false laws of heretics,
Against craft of idolatry,
Against spells of witches and smiths and wizards,
Against every knowledge that corrupts man's body
  and soul.
Christ to shield me today
Against poison, against burning,
Against drowning, against wounding,
So that there may come to me abundance of reward.

Christ with me, Christ before me, Christ behind me,
Christ in me, Christ beneath me, Christ above me,
Christ on my right, Christ on my left,
Christ when I lie down, Christ when I sit down, Christ
  when I arise,
Christ in the heart of every man who thinks of me,
Christ in the mouth of everyone who speaks of me,
Christ in every eye that sees me,
Christ in every ear that hears me.

I arise today
Through a mighty strength, the invocation of the
  Trinity,

Through belief in the threeness,
Through confession of the oneness,
Of the Creator of Creation.

66. I am nothing

I am nothing;
You are everything.
As you become greater,
Make me even less.

67. Come, Holy Spirit

Come, Holy Spirit:
Come into my morning, my day, my night;
Permeate my thoughts and infiltrate my speech;
Repaint me, inside and out.

Come, Holy Spirit:
Come into every area I might try to shut you out of;
Revolutionize my relationships and refocus my heart;
Repair me, inside and out.

68. To serve you as you deserve

Teach us, good Lord,
to serve you as you deserve,
to give and not to count the cost,
to fight and not to heed the wounds,
to toil and not to seek for rest,
to labour and not to ask for any reward,
save that of knowing that we do your will.
Amen.

St Ignatius of Loyola (1491–1556)

69. Teach me to let go

I know I am too quick to take charge,
Too keen to stay in control of my life.
Letting go feels almost beyond me.
Teach me, then, to let go.
When the future seems uncertain,
When I can't understand what you are doing and why,
Help me to learn to trust you.
May I grow a hard-wearing faith,
And know that, whatever is happening,
You are in control, and working for my good.

70. Thirsty for you

Like an animal in search of water,
My soul is thirsty for you, God.
I hunger for a real connection with you;
I am impatient to know you better.
Something deep inside me calls out to you,
Like a homing beacon buried within.
So many people around me don't believe –
They think I'm a fool for following you.
Yet I don't just believe; I know it on a primal level;
You are God, and I long to know you better.

Based on Psalm 42

71. Prayer for wisdom

God, I want to be wise.
Wise enough to settle arguments between friends;
Wise enough to know right from wrong, even when
    the line seems blurred;

Wise enough to see the bigger picture;
Wise enough to know which battles to pick;
Wise enough to know what love means in every
    situation;
Wise enough to see where you are at work all
    around me.
Give me the wisdom that enables all these things, God;
Give me wisdom, and teach me how to use it.

72. All I need

Of your goodness, O God, give yourself to me, for
you are sufficient for all my needs. Though I am not
worthy to receive you, I cannot ask for anything less.
Without you I shall always be in want. In you alone do
I have all I need, now and for ever.

Amen.

Julian of Norwich (1342–1416)

73. Help me to pray

Forgive me, God, for my silence;
My words so often dry up when I know they should
    flow easily.
Help me to pray; teach me how to talk to you as if you
    were standing in front of me.

74. In doubt

Though I've walked with you for a while, God,
I sometimes find myself doubting;
Doubting much more than I'd ever want to admit.
Forgive me my doubts, God;

Speak to me in my time of confusion;
Meet me even when I'm struggling to hear your voice.
Meet me *especially* when I'm struggling to hear your
  voice.

75.   O Holy Spirit

Breathe in me, O Holy Spirit,
that my thoughts may all be holy;
Act in me, O Holy Spirit,
that my work, too, may be holy;
Draw my heart, O Holy Spirit,
that I love but what is holy;
Strengthen me, O Holy Spirit,
to defend all that is holy;
Guard me, then, O Holy Spirit,
that I always may be holy.

Amen.

St Augustine of Hippo (354–430)

76.   For passion

I ask, God, that you would enlarge my heart,
And fill me with passion for the life you've called
  me to:
To serve my friends and my neighbours,
To live like I mean it,
To love you as you deserve.
Give me the passion to run head first into each day,
With eyes on you, and arms open wide.

77. Prayer of maturity and grace

Lord,
help me not to despise or oppose
what I do not understand.

William Penn (1644–1718)

78. Your word, our light

O Lord, you have given us your word for a light to
shine upon our path; grant us so to meditate on that
word, and follow its teaching, that we may find in it
the light that shines more and more until the perfect
day.

St Jerome (347–420)

79. For resilience

Make me resilient, God,
Give me a faith that lasts,
That survives the knocks.
When things go wrong, or don't work out,
May I know you still.
Place in me a quiet but undeniable knowledge of you,
So that, whatever comes, I will always say:
My God endures.

80. For love

Good Jesus, Fountain of Love,
Fill me with your love.
Absorb me into your love;
Compass me with your love,

That I may see all things in the light of your love,
Receive all things as the token of your love,
Speak of all things in words breathing of your love,
Win (through your love) others for your love,
Shine out each day with a new glow of your love,
Until I should enter into your everlasting love,
To adore your love, and love to adore you, my God
   and all.
Even so come, O Lord Jesus.

Based on a prayer by Edward Pusey (1800–82)

81. Make me generous

God, you love a cheerful giver;
Fill me with a passionate generosity.
Give to me, so that I might give to my friends;
Receive my giving as an act of worship.

Amen.

82. Redeemer, Friend and Brother

Thanks be to you, our Lord Jesus Christ,
for all the benefits which you have given us,
for all the pains and insults which you have borne
   for us.
Most merciful Redeemer, Friend and Brother,
may we know you more clearly,
love you more dearly,
and follow you more nearly,
day by day.

St Richard of Chichester (1197–1253)

83. All yours

The whole world is yours, God.

It's all yours!

Everything in it: everything that lives, everything that
    we can possess;

All of it comes from your hands.

Can I approach this God, who oversees everything?

If my hands are clean and my heart is pure,

And if I trust in you, then, incredibly – yes!

So I dare to walk towards you, and, as I do, I know
    your hand on my life.

How incredible – that the King of glory draws me
    near.

Based on Psalm 24

84. Fisherman's prayer

Lord, the sea is so wide
and my boat is so small.
Be with me.

Anonymous fisherman

85. You are fire

You are the Divine Spirit:
give me courage against all evil.
You are Fire:
enkindle in me your love.
You are Light:
enlighten my mind with the knowledge of eternal
    things.
You are the Dove:

give me innocence of life.
You are the gentle Breeze:
disperse the storms of my passions.
You are the Tongue:
teach me how to bless you always.
You are the Cloud:
shelter me under the shadow of your protection.

And, lastly, you are the giver of all heavenly gifts:
animate me, I ask you, with your grace;
sanctify me with your charity;
enlighten me with your wisdom;
adopt me by your goodness as your son,
and save me in your infinite mercy;
so that I may ever bless you, praise you, and love you;
first during this life on earth,
and then in heaven for all eternity.

Amen.

Based on a prayer by Alphonsus Liguori (1696–1787)

86. Walk to run

As I walk the journey of life,
Stumbling, tripping, careering along,
Please keep my feet on solid ground,
Make my paths straight,
And receive me as I run into your arms.

87. Anima Christi

Soul of Christ, sanctify me,
Body of Christ, save me,
Blood of Christ, inebriate me,

Water from the side of Christ, wash me,
Passion of Christ, strengthen me.
O good Jesus, hear me.
Within Thy wounds hide me,
Permit me not to be separated from Thee,
From the malicious enemy defend me.
In the hour of my death call me
And bid me come unto Thee,
That with thy Saints I may praise Thee,
For ever and ever.

Fourteenth-century prayer

88. Love lasts for ever

I am so thankful to you, God, because of your
    goodness;
You love me, and that love lasts an eternal lifetime.
Through your Son you have rescued me;
Through calling out to me, you have drawn me close;
Even though I was far away, you reached out your
    hand and I took it.
Just like generations of your children,
You have led me out of the life I used to live,
And brought me into a place of safety.
Just as you heard their cries, you have heard mine.
So I am full of thanks and praise,
Because your love never stops or even slows down.
It's the same today as it was ten thousand years ago,
The same as it will be for all of time.

Based on Psalm 107

89. Jesus loves me

This beautiful old hymn (slightly edited) refers to Jesus' words in Mark 10:16, where he invites children to join him when the disciples would have kept them away. The words, and these verses, challenge us to make sure that, in one sense at least, our faith always remains childlike – taking Jesus completely at his word, and running into his arms at every opportunity. Although this was written as a hymn, it also makes for a perfect prayer as we recommit daily to following Jesus in this way.

Jesus loves me! This I know,
For the Bible tells me so.
Little ones to Him belong;
They are weak, but He is strong.

Jesus loves me! This I know,
As He loved so long ago,
Taking children on His knee,
Saying, "Let them come to Me."

Jesus loves me still today,
Walking with me on my way,
Wanting as a friend to give
Light and love to all who live.

Jesus loves me! He who died
Heaven's gate to open wide;
He will wash away my sin,
Let His little child come in.

Jesus loves me! He will stay
Close beside me all the way;
Thou hast bled and died for me,
I will ever live for Thee.

Anna Bartlett Warner (1827–1915)

90. All through this day

All through this day, O Lord, by the power of your quickening Spirit, let me touch the lives of others for good, whether through the words I speak, the prayer I breathe, or the life I live.

Amen.

Anon.

91. Sick, hungry, needy

Trusting in your goodness
and great mercy, Lord, I come:
sick – I come to my Saviour;
hungry and thirsty – to the well of Life;
needy – to the King of heaven.

Thomas à Kempis (1380–1471)

92. Teach us to pray

Teach us, O God, to pray as our Saviour taught his disciples. As we come into your presence, give us humble and repentant hearts, conscious of our deep unworthiness, of our unutterable need, and of your power to help us. Grant us wisdom to watch for your answers, and the grace to thank you for every gift you give, knowing that, loving us as your children, you will provide for all our needs; through Jesus Christ our Lord.

Amen.

Traditional Anglican prayer

93. Closer than breath

Lord, you are closer to me
than my own breathing,
nearer than my hands and feet.

St Teresa of Avila (1515–82)

94. Like a child

God our heavenly Father,
when the thought of you
wakes in our hearts,
let its awakening
not be like a startled bird
that flies about in fear.
Instead, let it be like a child
waking from sleep
with a heavenly smile.

Søren Kierkegaard (1813–55)

95. Beyond the natural

Allow me to perceive things as they really are, God;
Where angels and demons operate unseen,
Give me spiritual eyes to tell natural from
    supernatural.
When all is not as it seems, give me insight,
And the wisdom to know how to pray and what to do.

96. Grow my faith

Grow my faith, God,
Strengthen my resolve to serve others.
Work through my hands and my feet,
Bless the words that come out of my mouth,
This and every day.

97. Enlarge my dreams

Give me bigger dreams, God;
Turn my ambitions to you – then double them.
Fill my head with vision and stir me up to think
   bigger;
Breathe faith into my ideas.
I want to be a dreamer for you.

98. Temptation

Lord Jesus, you know everything about me.
There's nothing hidden from you; I know you see
   right into my heart.
You know all my thoughts – both good and wrong.
It scares me: you see the ways I long to love you more
   and serve you better,
But you also see the things I struggle with,
The battles I fight, and the things that tempt me away
   from being who I should be.

Forgive me again, Lord, and help me to stand firm
against the things that seek to draw me away from
you.

Lord, when my thoughts and feet wander to where
they shouldn't be, please turn me around and help me
to come back to you.

When I see and hear things that are not helpful in
making me more like you, help me to realize it and
walk away from them.

I long to be obedient to you, but I can't do it on
   my own.
Please help me be the person you want me to be.

Laura Haddow

99. Purify my heart

I desire a pure heart,
A holiness that mirrors, in some dulled and imperfect
   way,
The gloriousness of my Saviour.
Lord, purify my heart;
Iron out the imperfections in my character;
May others see an impression of Jesus, even in me.

100. Teach me where to find you

O Lord my God,
teach my heart this day
where and how to find you.
You have made me and re-made me,
and you have bestowed on me
all the good things I possess,
and still I do not know you.
I have not yet done
that for which I was made.

Teach me to seek you,
for I cannot seek you
unless you teach me,
or find you
unless you show yourself to me.
Let me seek you in my desire;
let me desire you in my seeking.
Let me find you by loving you;
let me love you when I find you.

St Anselm (1033–1109)

101. All worship

May my whole life be an act of worship, Lord,
To you: the one who made me and gives me life.
As much on the sports field as in the chapel;
As much in my conversation as when you and I
   are alone.
May everything I do point heavenward;
May every word I say make you smile.
Teach me to worship you with everything I do,
Everything I say,
Everything I am.

102. Abandoned into his hands

Father,
I abandon myself into your hands;
do with me what you will.
Whatever you may do, I thank you:
I am ready for all, I accept all.
Let only your will be done in me
and in all your creatures.

I wish no more than this, O Lord.
Into your hands I commend my soul:
I offer it to you
with all the love of my heart,
for I love you, Lord,
and so need to give myself,
to surrender myself into your hands
without reserve,
and with boundless confidence,
for you are my Father.

Charles de Foucauld (1858–1916)

103. God my guide

Guide me, God,
Be my map, my inbuilt navigation system;
Direct my life,
Make my routes direct, and keep me from getting lost.
Show me, God,
Where to go, what to do, which paths to choose;
Light my way.
Don't let me journey alone, but with you as my
    constant companion.

104. Each morning broken

*This prayer is a little harsh, and also a little strange – reminding us of
Paul's words in 1 Corinthians 15:31: "I die every day – I mean that,
brothers – just as surely as I glory over you in Christ Jesus our Lord."
In this verse, Paul may have been referring to the fact that he could
have been killed for his faith at any time, but he also means that, each
day, he makes the decision to put God's plans first and himself last.
These brief words by a Danish theologian and philosopher are a call for*

*us to follow Paul and put the same principle to work in our own lives –
dying to ourselves each day as we put God first.*

> Lord! Make my heart your temple in which you live.
> Grant that every impure thought, every earthly desire
> might be like the idol Dagon – each morning broken at
> the feet of the Ark of the Covenant. Teach us to master
> flesh and blood, and let this mastery of ourselves be
> our bloody sacrifice, in order that we might be able to
> say with the Apostle: "I die every day."
>
> Søren Kierkegaard (1813–55)

105. Increase/decrease

> You must increase,
> I must decrease.
> You must become greater,
> I must become less.
> Teach me, Lord God,
> To love putting myself last.

106. For truthfulness

> When I look around me at the pain that is often caused
>   by lies,
> Unfaithfulness,
> Gossip,
> And rumours,
> It makes me realize the importance of truthfulness.
>
> As I long to be a person who radiates you
> In all parts of my life,
> I pray you will help me to grow in truth and honesty.

You know every word before I speak it;
Help me to control the things I say to others,
To make me more aware that words are powerful and
    can often be harmful.

Help me to see
That there is no such thing as a white lie;
All lies are destructive, no matter how big or small
    they seem to us.

My desire is to be a person who reflects you in all your
    ways.

Please continue to change me and mould me into who
    you want me to be.

Amen.

107. Serenity, courage and wisdom

I have loved this since the first time I ever heard it – it's the sort of simple prayer that often finds its way onto bookmarks and coffee mugs. Even if it is familiar, enjoy it again – in just a few words is contained great wisdom for anyone hoping to develop their character.

God grant me
the serenity to accept the things I cannot change,
the courage to change the things I can,
and the wisdom
to distinguish the one from the other.

Reinhold Niebuhr (1892–1971)

108. Sanctuary

You to me, God, are a sanctuary,
A place of rest and calm.
You give me a place to rest my head,
When the world is moving too fast
And evil is all around me.
You, Lord, are a sanctuary for my soul.

Based on Psalm 11

109. Fill this empty vessel

Look, Lord,
on an empty vessel that needs to be filled.
In faith I am weak – strengthen me.
In love I am cold – warm me and make me fervent
so that my love may go out to my neighbour.
I doubt and am unable to trust you completely.
Lord, strengthen my faith and trust in you.
You are all the treasure I possess.
I am poor, you are rich,
and you came to have mercy on the poor.
I am a sinner, you are goodness.
From you I can receive goodness,
but I can give you nothing.
Therefore I shall stay with you.

Martin Luther

110. For patience

Dear Lord,
As I live in a culture that moves and changes so fast,
Where we are used to finding instant answers to our
  questions,

Teach me how to be patient;
Teach my heart to be content in waiting for you to
    answer my prayers in your time – and not mine.
Help me to draw away from the busyness of life
And learn to be quiet – alone with you.
Remind me when I forget,
That when I don't get instant answers from you
It's not because you've forgotten
But because your timing is perfect
And your ways are always best for me.
Please help my heart to be still and wait upon you.

Laura Haddow

111. Realization of power

Lord, the Lover of Souls,
Forgive us for so often looking on the limitations of
    our lives,
Instead of realizing their limitless power in your
    power;
Forgive us all for our incomprehensible slowness in
    making use of that power,
Power which you have handed to us,
Through Jesus Christ our Saviour.

Based on a prayer by Lucy H. M. Soulsby (1856–1927)

112. Little things and great

Teach us, Lord,
to do little things
as though they were great
because of the majesty of Christ

who does them in us,
and who lives our life.
Teach us to do the greatest things
as though they were little and easy,
because of his omnipotence.

Blaise Pascal (1623–62)

113. I will chase after you

There really is a God
– And I will chase after you.
Deep within me there is a longing,
A need to be close to you.
As long as I live, I will keep walking towards you,
Praising you, worshipping you;
Day and night I will think of you,
Each step I take will be in your direction.

Based on Psalm 63

The following prayers are based on others written by the amazing German theologian Dietrich Bonhoffer. They provide great bookends for a day – and remind us of our total dependence on God.

114. Prayer for the start of the day

At the beginning of the day Lord, I call to you.
Help me to pray,
Help me concentrate on you.
You know this is hard for me –
There is darkness in me that tries to cloud my view
    of you;
Yet in you there is light.
Without you I am alone, but you don't leave me;
Without you I am weak, but you help me;

Without you I am restless, but you bring peace;
Without you I am short-tempered, but help me to
  be patient;
I don't fully understand you Lord,
But I know you understand me completely.
Restore me this morning,
Give me the strength I will need for today,
So that I might serve you and those around me.
Whatever today might bring Lord,
Your name be praised.

Based on a prayer by Dietrich Bonhoeffer (1906–45)

115. Prayer for the end of the day

Lord God,
Thank you for seeing me through this day.
Thank you for the chance to rest now –
Body and soul.
You have been with me, alongside me, even working
  through me;
You have guided and watched over me.
Forgive me for when my faith has been weak today.
Forgive me for all the things I have done wrong today,
And give me the strength to forgive those who have
  wronged me.
Now Lord, I pray you would give me deep and
  restful sleep,
And protect me and all those who I love
May I rise again tomorrow to serve you once more,
But until then, I will end this day by saying:
God – your holy name be praised.

Based on a prayer by Dietrich Bonhoeffer (1906–45)

Pain

There are moments when even the most staunch atheists consider turning to prayer, and very often there is a common reason. In times of fear, sickness and pain, we are most keenly aware of just how small and helpless we are, and of how big (and often insurmountable) our problems seem. When we're worried about something, when we realize that things aren't in our control, we often turn to God. Whether that's when a family member is desperately ill, or simply because we feel deeply disappointed that a situation isn't turning out the way we'd hoped, the words just seem to flow out of us. I don't know about you, but I find it much easier to pray about the things I'm concerned about than to pray prayers of thanks and praise for things that have already turned out well. Is that a problem for God? I don't think so – look at the Bible, most notably the books of Psalms and Lamentations, and the story of Job.

God wants to know every part of us, and he loves it that we draw close to him when we tell him about the things that are on our mind. Of course, as Jesus models it in Matthew 6, a really healthy prayer life mixes confession, praise, thanksgiving and request, but we should never feel guilty for praying in just one of these ways. God loves it when we come to him in prayer – he just adores it when his children connect with him. And the most amazing thing (and perhaps another reason why we often turn to prayer when all else fails) is that God doesn't just hear our prayers – he answers them too. Sometimes not exactly how we'd like, but, so often, in ways that startle and amaze us. He brings healing to the sick, comfort to the grieving, peace to the fearful. Whatever the answer to our prayers might be, we can know one thing for sure: that God understands pain. The Father we pray to is the same God who watched his Son tortured and killed in the most inhuman way. The Jesus we pray through felt every crack of the whip, every last drive of the nails as he was crucified. Whatever we're struggling with, suffering, or feeling, he understands. He has been there.

EMOTIONAL PAIN AND SUFFERING

116. Everyone vs me

God, I feel like everyone is against me;
Like everything is stacking up, backing me into a
   corner.
You are the only one I can call to for help,
And yet I know that you have it all in hand;
You will not let me be beaten,
Because you are my Father and I am your child.
You watch over me; you are my rescuer and my
   shelter.

Based on Psalm 2

117. Here with me

Lord, thank you that you are here with me,
That even though I'm in a dark place right now
I know that your arms are around me
And that I'm not alone.
Please help me to keep trusting you;
When the doubts start creeping in,
Please chase them away.
Keep my eyes focused upon yours and give me
strength to face another day.

Laura Haddow

118. Inexpressible

My pain is inexpressible, Lord.
Thank you that I do not need to be able to form words
For you to be able to hear me.

119. Darkness

People tell me I have nothing to worry about;
They don't know the first thing about me.
When it's really bad, I can barely see through the
darkness, the fog.
It hangs over me and I can't do anything to disperse it.
I believe that you know what's going on in my head;
I hope and trust that you have a good plan for my
future.
Bring a light to me, Lord.

120. Struggling with self-esteem

At times when I feel ugly,
Help me to see myself in the way that you do.

When I look at my life and feel I have nothing to offer,
Remind me that, even though they may be small,
You have given me gifts.
Help me to find them inside myself and use them
   for you.

When I feel worthless and insignificant,
Show me afresh the wonder of the cross,
The place where you died for me
Because you loved me so much.

When I feel alone,
Remind me that the creator of the universe is always
   with me
And that the Holy Spirit lives inside me
And that although I may feel I'm alone
It could not be further from the truth.

When I feel scared about the future,
Help me remember
That all my days are held within your hands,
That you know my dreams and hopes
And have great plans for me.

When I feel like giving up,
Help me to think about heaven
And motivate me to carry on.
Remind me of the amazing future I will get to spend
   with you
Where there will be no more tears,
No more fear or suffering,

In a place so beautiful it will never cease to amaze me,
And, most importantly,
Where I will be with you for ever...

Anon.

121. For wounded souls

Loving Jesus, enfold in your compassion, those who are ill in body, mind, or soul. Lay a healing hand upon the wounds of their souls, that inner peace may be their portion. Revive their failing strength and let life conquer death in their suffering bodies, that, rejoicing in your mercy, they may serve you with grateful hearts all their days upon earth.

Amen.

Traditional Anglican prayer

122. For a struggling friend

Lord, to my friend who is struggling at the moment
I ask that you would bring peace.
Though he feels defeated,
Would he find new strength in you;
Though the path ahead looks bleak to him,
Would you begin to show him a way through.
Even more than that, Lord, would you help him to see
How deeply he is loved by his friends,
How much we want to help him.
Bring him out of this fog, Lord;
Nurse him back to his former health.

123. Your will be done

Lord God, in a situation I neither like nor understand, may your will be done. I ask that, by your grace, I would know the privilege and reassurance of seeing just a little of your plan, which works for my good, even in the dark times. Help me to say again, even when the pain is most severe, "Your will be done."

124. Can you hear me?

Where are you, God?
Can you hear me?
Please listen to me,
Please answer my prayers.
I believe you are there, listening;
I ask that you'll soothe the pain I'm feeling.
I ask for joy. I ask for peace.
I ask for rest in you.

Based on Psalm 4

125. I wouldn't have chosen this

Heavenly Father,

I know that at the same time as you hold galaxies in
    place by the power of your hand,
You also control the beat of my heart.

I am made and known completely by you.
And at times like now, when I struggle to understand
why things are the way they are; why sometimes the
road you choose for me to walk down is painful and
hard,

I know that you are God;
I know that you love me, and I can trust you,
That the plans you have for me are to strengthen my
faith and make me more like you.

So even when the ways you choose for me
are not what I would have chosen for myself,
Help me to face them, knowing that all my days are in
your hands.

Laura Haddow

WHEN WE DON'T LIKE OURSELVES

126. How you know me

You know me so well.
You watch over me constantly; you see everything
    I do.
I am so familiar to you that you know what I'm about
    to say before I even say it.
Wherever I go, you are in the space immediately in
    front of me,
And at the same time you're in the place I've just been.
I can never run away from you.
Anywhere I go, you are there –
Whether I go to the depths of the sea
Or the summit of a mountain,
You're already there; you've always been there.
So how amazing it is to think about my creation,
And the hand you had in it;
Because you stitched me together;
Inside my mother's womb your hands brought the
    divine spark that gave me life.

I am "fearfully and wonderfully made";
I worship you, God, because you made me.
When I find it hard to love myself I remember that I
  am your handiwork,
And that you do not make mistakes.

Based on Psalm 139

127. Nothing right

God, I feel like nothing is going right,
As if every step I take becomes a stumble.
I feel useless,
Like I'm setting myself up to fail in everything I do.
God, help me not to feel like this,
And help me to know that, even when I fail, you still
  delight in me;
That there is nothing I can do to make you love me
  more,
And nothing I can do to make you love me less.

128. Hard to love myself

God, if I loved my neighbours as I love myself,
My neighbours might not appreciate it.
I don't like me;
If I were my own friend, I'd disown me.
I cannot see anything attractive, likeable or interesting
  in my personality;
I can't bear to look in the mirror.
I want to see myself as you see me,
But right now all I see is ugliness.
Please draw near to me, Lord, and help me to like
  myself.

129. Believing the bullies

This prayer may be helpful if you have suffered from bullying or teasing, and are starting to believe the unkind words that have been spoken over you.

> When people mock me, perhaps they have a point;
> There must be a reason why they pick on me.
> I know I have my flaws; perhaps I deserve it.
> Yet you don't see me like that;
> You love me unconditionally as your child –
> When you look at me you can't help breaking into
>   a smile.
> Help me, God, especially when the bullies come,
> To know that truth deep inside,
> And to allow it to transform my thinking,
> So that somehow I might begin to see myself as you
>   see me.
> Amen.

130. Wrap your arms around me

> I feel cold in my own skin.
> God of love, wrap your arms around me.
>
> My life is a battle; each day I wade in again.
> God of love, wrap your arms around me.
>
> When I think about myself, I am repulsed.
> God of love, wrap your arms around me.
>
> When I think about you, I feel so unworthy.
> God of love, wrap your arms around me.

PHYSICAL PAIN

131. Hear my cry

God, who heard the cry of the Israelites in Egypt,
Hear me now as I call out to you.
I am suffering with pain, and while I know that others
    suffer even more greatly,
To me, now, this is hard to bear.
Please relieve me of this pain; please work in me
    supernaturally;
Bring me back to health by the power of your Spirit.
As I call out to you, I know that you hear me.
I ask that you would choose to take this pain away;
For the glory of your Son, Jesus Christ.

Amen.

132. Simple prayer for healing

God of incalculable power,
Please bring healing now.

133. To those who call on you

O God, who is always near to anyone who calls
    on you;
Who sent your Son into the world not only that we
    might have life, but that we might have it to the full;
Send your blessing upon us, your children, when we
    look to you for help.
In every hour of weakness and in every moment of
    pain, help us to be conscious of your presence and
    your love,

That we may feel surrounded with that peace of God
that passes all understanding.

Based on a traditional Anglican prayer

134. Miracles of God

God of healing,
Fill me with your Spirit,
That I might carry His power
To those in need of healing and restoration
And see, even in these days,
Miracles of God by my own hands.

135. Stand by their beds

Dear Heavenly Father, look on those
Who lie in weary pain.
O Saviour, stand beside their beds
And make them whole again.

Anon.

136. Lord in my pain

Though I suffer pain, Lord, you are greater than it,
You could make it disappear in an instant,
You could take it away with a word.
I pray that you would choose to heal me, but, if not,
Would you grow my character through suffering,
So that it might not be in vain
But make me into a closer likeness of Jesus.

137. For a right attitude towards pain

We ask you not, Lord, to rid us of pain;
But to grant in your mercy that our pain may be free
  from waste,

Free from rebellion against your will,
Free from thought of ourselves
And purified by love.

H. S. Nash

138. From strength to strength

Look after my health, Lord;
May I go from strength to strength.

139. Use even us

In a world full of hurt, Lord,
Use our frail, fumbling hands,
And our dim, stumbling faith,
And, through the miraculous input of your Holy
  Spirit,
Bring healing on every level to those in need of it.

140. For holistic healing

Living Christ,
Make us conscious now of your healing nearness.
Touch our eyes that we may see you;
Open our ears that we may hear your voice;
Enter our hearts that we may know your love.
Overshadow our souls and bodies with your presence,
That we may be filled with your strength,
Your love,
And your healing life.

Amen.

Traditional. Anon

GRIEF AND BEREAVEMENT

141. When someone has died

Lord,
welcome into your calm and peaceful kingdom
those who have departed out of this present life
to be with you.
Grant them rest
and a place with the spirits of the just;
and give them the life that knows no age,
the reward that passes not away,
through Christ our Lord.

Amen.

St Ignatius of Loyola (1491–1556)

142. Only darkness

God, in my moment of grief, I can see no light;
Only darkness.
Inhabit my suffering, Lord; illuminate my path;
Lead me towards a new day.

143. No understanding

My heart has sunk into a new, terrible place;
I feel sick to the stomach;
My mind is not capable of understanding;
God of love, wrap your arms around me.

My soul is pervaded by a dull ache;
I cannot put my hands to any useful work;
There are no words to express my grief;
God of love, wrap your arms around me.

144. God, my hiding place

When the pain of this world has almost snuffed
  me out,
Lord, you are my hiding place; you have rescued me,
  and given me shelter in the storm.
You are a firm rock on which I can stand;
You are a fortress that surrounds and protects me.
I will trust in you – you who know the anguish in
  my soul,
You see, know and feel my pain; you have compassion
  for me;
In this time of distress, when my body and soul are
  weak, you are there;
You hold me up when I can barely stand.

Based on Psalm 31

145. In the loss of a friend

God, bless the family of my friend;
Enfold them with your love and peace.
May your unmistakable warmth radiate through our
  community;
And may you help us all to make sense of our loss and
  grief.
God, who brings hope when all hope seems lost,
Be with us no less tomorrow than you are today.

DIVORCE

This small collection of prayers is written for use if you, or someone close to you, are being affected by divorce or separation. These times can be devastating for everyone involved – and certainly not just for the couple at the epicentre of the situation.

146. Misunderstood

No one understands how I'm feeling;
How can they?
Nobody has ever been me, going through this before.
When I try to express myself, the words come out
  wrong;
I can't even articulate my hurt.
God, who doesn't need me to have the right words,
Please understand me and comfort me now.

147. For reconciliation

Even though I know the chance is slim,
Even after all that has already happened,
I still ask that this separation could be reversed,
That this relationship could be restored.

Even though it seems beyond us now,
Even after every word that has been spoken,
I still come to you, Healer God, and ask you to heal
  this rift,
Pull them back, even from the brink, if it's your will.

148. Bring peace

To a family in crisis,
I pray, Lord, you would bring peace.

To tongues primed for harsh words,
I pray you would bring stillness.
To difficult conversations,
I pray you would bring grace.
To all of us, feeling hurt and helpless,
I pray you would draw near.

149. For my parents

At this time, God, even and especially as I am finding them difficult, I lift my parents to you in prayer, and ask you to bless them, comfort them, and, in whatever way possible, draw them closer together, so that they might know peace, civility, and, most of all, your arms around them both.

Amen.

150. Angry

God, I'm angry.
I see red every time I think about it.
Other people try to help; more often they make me
    angrier still without trying.
I want to run into the middle of a field and scream.
Help me, God, to be angry in the right way, and only
    about the right things;
Give me patience with those who love me,
Peace to overcome my fury,
And a closer and deeper knowledge of you, here by
    my side through all of it.

DOUBT

*These prayers are here to be used whenever we have doubts in our faith.
They are perfectly healthy – even Jesus' own disciples struggled with
doubt, and they could see him in the flesh! The important thing is that
we process and wrestle with doubt properly, and these next prayers
offer us an opportunity to do that. Some of them refer to small, niggling
concerns; others deal with full-blown doubt about God's existence.
Whatever you're feeling, it is OK, and can be a very positive thing.
Spend some time in prayer, and use this as a starting point.*

151. Confused

I find myself completely confused;
God, bring insight, wisdom, and a greater knowledge
　of you.
Shine a light inside my head where I just don't get it –
I want to understand you better.

152. Doubting everything

Are you even there, God?
I accept it may be me, but I just can't see you right
　now.
If you are real, you are the most important thing in the
　universe;
If you're not real, I'm really wasting my time.
So even though I'm just one person in a race of
　billions,
I ask that you would make yourself known to me
　again.
I think you're there, God –
Please confirm my suspicions.

153. Kept awake

God, my doubts keep me awake at night;
Please give me reassurance, peace, and sleep.

154. Guilty about doubt

God, I feel like such a fraud;
I speak of you, and yet I doubt you.
Please help me to address my doubts,
And to speak from a place of certain hope.
Please also address my guilt;
Assure me that my doubts don't threaten or anger you;
Give me an intellect that thinks clearly,
And a mind that remains receptive to you.

155. Small problem

There are small, niggling things that I don't understand about you, Lord; about your word, your story and your people. They lurk right in the background, but occasionally they rear their heads up and make me stumble. Help me to deal with them; teach me to ask questions, instead of trying to bottle them up. Where answers are possible, I pray they'd be given to me, and where it's just more complicated than that, I pray you'd walk with me as I try to reach some kind of peace.

Amen.

156. Subtle difference

Give me the maturity, Lord,
to ask you questions

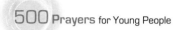

Rather than, each time I struggle,
questioning you.

Anon.

157. Regarding suffering

I don't understand, God,
Why it seems you allow bad things to happen to good
  people.
My heart is open, but I'm scratching my head;
Please make this painful mystery a little clearer to me,
That I might know for myself,
And be able to encourage others.

158. Why trust the Bible?

If the Bible was written by clever men alone, then my
  faith is a sham.
If the words I'm asked to live by aren't God-breathed
  at all, it all falls apart.
So, God, I ask you to give me a deeper understanding
  of your word:
How it was put together,
How it hangs together,
How you are right at the heart of it,
And how, in a way I don't really understand, this can
  be a "living word".
I want to be a student and a lover of the Scriptures;
Help me to overcome my doubts with both faith and
  reasoned judgment,
And lead me into a lifelong connection with the Bible
  which totally transforms me.

159. Struggling with Scripture

Lord, there are parts of your word that, to my mind right now, seem inconsistent, confusing, or even contradictory. Help me to see and understand the big picture of your character and your story, that I might know you better and become a part of that same story myself.

Amen.

160. Unanswered prayer

God, I feel like you're not answering my prayers,
And yet you promise to.
What does that mean?
Am I not asking right?
Do I not have the right amount of faith?
Or have I missed your answer?
Please show me plainly, Lord.
Right now I'm just confused.
Even if the answer is no, I submit to your will,
But at the moment I can't hear any answer at all.
Forgive me and bear with me if I'm missing
    something;
Lord, in all humility I repeat my request to you.

DISAPPOINTMENT

161. To trust you again

Help me to trust in you again
Even though my heart is weighed down with
    questions

And I struggle to understand.
Help me still to praise you with everything I am,
Knowing that with you
There are no mistakes –
You are God;
And that behind every disappointment is a reason.
Thank you that you have a plan for my life.

162. Not as I'd hoped

You know this hasn't turned out as I had hoped;
You know my dreams seem to have been dashed.
Though I thought the signs looked so good,
My plans appear to have come to nothing.

Lord, comfort me in my moment of disappointment;
Remain close to me as I try to work out what went
  wrong.
Keep me from apportioning blame, and bring me back
  to a place where,
Whatever happens to my plans,
It is in yours that I place my trust completely.

163. Disappointed with God

*This prayer may be particularly appropriate when something in your
life hasn't worked out the way you'd hoped – and especially when you
thought God had spoken to you about it.*

God, I feel so low;
I thought I had heard you,
And now it seems I heard incorrectly.
Even though I know how this sounds:
I feel angry;
I feel disappointed;

I feel that you have let me down.
I know in my heart that you want only the best for me,
But it's hard to feel that in the midst of this.
Help me to see the bigger picture;
To know why this has happened;
To understand your plan better;
And to hear you more clearly.

Amen.

164. Response to unfairness

God, I see so many things that seem unfair.
How can I voice my frustration without hurting
   others?
How can I show my pain without causing distress?
Show me how to act wisely,
and give me your perspective.

Helen Crawford

165. In times of failure

Let me not pray to be sheltered from dangers,
but to be fearless in facing them.
Let me not beg for the stilling of my pain,
but for the heart to conquer it.
Let me not crave in anxious fear to be saved,
but hope for the patience to win my freedom.
Grant me that I may not be a coward,
feeling your mercy in my success alone,
but let me find the grasp of your hand
in my failure.

Rabindranath Tagore (1861–1941)

FEAR

166. Insomnia due to fear

I lie awake in the middle of the night;
Unable to sleep, I become consumed by fear.
Rationality and reason cannot help me;
Reassuring words do not affect me.
I need your help, Lord, to clear my mind,
To soothe my fearful thoughts,
To give me rest in you.

167. Consequences

You know, Lord, the mistakes I have made in my past.
I know that you have forgiven me completely;
Still I fear that my actions have consequences, which
    will hunt me down as I seek to move on with my life.
I cannot ask you to protect me from the cost of my
    actions,
But I will ask you to steady me for when it arrives to
    pay me back.
I will ask you to help me to deal with the fallout,
And I will trust you to remain by my side throughout
    it all.

168. Help me to stand

When my heart is filled with fear
and darkness closes in around me,
I will not be afraid,
For I know I am not alone.
When all I want is to run
From the situations that scare me so much,

Almighty God,
Help me to stand,
Not in my strength but in yours.
When my courage fades,
Remind me of your promise
That tells me you never leave my side,
Not for a second.
Who can hurt me, while you stand next to me?
I know you are always watching,
Always ready to defend me,
Always there.
In you I am safe for ever,
Sheltered under your wings,
Surrounded by your love.

169. When I encounter fear

When I encounter fear,
May I know instead the reassurance of your hand
  upon my shoulder;
Of your Spirit, whispering within me;
And of your word, leading me back into the light.

Amen.

170. Recurring worry

You know the thing I always worry about, God,
That same old recurring concern that won't go away.
Lord, I ask that you would break the power of my
  fears,
That you'd smash the cycle of worry,
So that I might be able to stare my monster down,
And, with you as my protector and my guide,
Step forward into a life liberated from fear.

CONSIDERING HARM

171. Rock bottom

Even to stand up at this moment
I would have to scrape myself off rock bottom.
I have no further to fall;
It feels as if my life has shattered into a million pieces.
Though it horrifies me even to think it,
Ending it all actually seems like an option.
I cannot see another way out of the mire I've waded
   into.
So, God, if you are there,
Shine a light on me.
If you love me,
Throw me a rope.
I never wanted to end up here.
Please come and rescue me.

172. Help!

God, you know how I'm feeling;
All knotted up inside, like I'm suffocating.
I don't want to do something stupid,
But the thought keeps crossing my mind.
Before I hurt myself,
Please send me someone who can help.

173. Harmer's prayer

*This prayer is intended for someone caught in a cycle of self-harm. For
help and information on this topic, visit www.selfharm.co.uk*

God, you know my secret agony,
And the lengths I go to, to try to ease it.

To erase pain I embrace pain;
In the aftermath, relief and shame come rushing
  together.
Though I hurt myself, and injure you,
Lord, please do not remove yourself from me,
But instead bring wholeness, bring healing,
Restore me outside and in.
I ask it very humbly, in Jesus' name.

Amen.

174. Help me to stop

Help me to stop, Lord;
Give me the strength of mind,
Give me the distractions and the circumstances
That prevent me from ending up there again.
Instead of a rush of endorphins,
Flood me with the transforming power of your Spirit,
So that I might be healed and renewed, in body and
  in soul.

175. A prayer of hope

Lord, you know me; you know every hair on my head.
Lord, you love me; you sent your Son to die for me.
Lord, you know my pain; your Son became fully
  human for me.
Lord, you understand me; your Spirit lives within me.
Lord, you rescue me; you hear my cry and answer it.
Lord, you restore me; you lead me into the light.

Intercession

Intercession is a very "religious" word, but I use it because I think it best sums up the point of this next section. It literally means "to stand in the gap" – between God and someone or something that needs His intervention – and pray on behalf of that person or situation. We are naturally very good at praying for ourselves. If a problem or a difficult situation arises right in front of us, a prayer may often be the natural response. We're usually less good at seeing the need for prayer in a situation that doesn't directly involve us. We might then respond by feeling sad, giving advice, or just talking to other people about it. Our instinct for prayer is less strong. Sometimes we might say to a friend: "I'll pray for you," but even then the promise doesn't actually translate into a prayer. We may see images of war-torn or poverty-stricken countries on the TV news and momentarily feel terrible; we might be handed a leaflet asking us to pray for Christians persecuted in far-flung places; even then, we may never get around to the time-consuming practice of prayer. The simple reason is that it doesn't directly involve us.

So these prayers are a tool to help us kick back against our natural self-obsession, and underline to God how much we care about his world; how seriously we take Jesus' call to "love one another" in every sense, including the spiritual. After all, do we believe that prayer works, or not? If the answer is yes, then taking time to pray for the hurting, the broken and the oppressed isn't just a sign of spiritual health – it's a responsibility.

FOR THOSE WHO DON'T KNOW YOU

176. Prayer for revival

We're not very good at dreaming big;
Too often a part of us just accepts things as they are.
Yet, when we know you, we realize that your heart
    and your concern extend to everyone.
You love us all; you sent your Son to die for us all,
So, Lord, we dare to ask that you would revive your
    church again,
That you would turn the culture of this country upside
    down with shockwaves of love,
That we would see hundreds in our towns, thousands
    in our cities, and millions in our nation turning their
    back on the "wisdom of the world" and turning
    to you.
Just as your love reaches even to the last and the least
    of us,
So, Lord, would you bring an entire generation back
    to you.
In Jesus' name, through which we are allowed to
    dream this big, we pray.

Amen.

177. Start with me

Lord, send revival,
Start with me.

Anon.

178. Prayer for atheists

There are some who say they hate your name;
Who deny you, even with the breath you have given
them.
You could choose to silence them, but you let them
live;
Your amazing love is so much bigger.
I pray for those in our society who are like Saul,
And ask that you might shine your light of love into
their lives
So that they have no choice but to turn 180°,
And become the Pauls of this age.

Amen.

179. For celebrities and influencers

On the famous, the beloved and the influential figures
of my nation,
I pray you would send your blessing;
And I ask that some who have a voice to which many
listen
Would come to know you as their Saviour,
That through your influence working through them
Many would come to know you.
For sportsmen and -women,
For actors, musicians and writers,
For politicians and public figures

I pray, asking you to break into their hearts right now;
Asking you to call them by name;
Asking you to soften their hearts;
Asking you to draw them to yourself.

180. For myself

Lord Jesus, I know that I don't know you personally.
I've never made the leap of faith that's involved in
    really trusting you.
But I want to; I want to know the God who built the
    universe, personally.
I want to thank the Jesus who died for me, and
    become his friend.
Please enter into my heart – whatever that means in
    practice;
Please forgive me for anything I've ever done that's
    wronged you or let you down.
Be my helper and my guide, for the rest of my life,
And welcome me into eternity when I reach its end.

FOR MY LOCAL CHURCH

181. More than a building

God, may this church be more than a building;
More than just a group of individuals;
More than just prayers and songs on a Sunday.
Instead, may it be a source of hope and
    transformation,
Through which you turn this community upside
    down with love.

182. For my church leaders

Lord God,
I lift to you the leaders of my church,
And ask that you would inspire them and encourage
  them.
Comfort them when they feel weak;
When they feel empty, give them your wisdom.
Fill them continually with your Holy Spirit, and be the
  driving force inside them;
And, as they lead us, lead them into a closer walk
  with you.

183. A church that takes us seriously

God, I pray that our church might be one that hears
  the voice of youth,
And seeks to understand it;
That takes seriously our needs and also our dreams for
  the future.
Lord, make this a church that places young people at
  the heart of the action,
And in doing so draws many more to you.

184. Community impact

In a community with so many needs, with so many
  hurting people,
We the church are your Plan A.
There is no Plan B.
Help us, then, to live up to the responsibility with
  which you've entrusted us,
To be good news to the poor,
To be bringers of your kingdom.

Show us how to have an impact on this community;
That it might see your love in us,
And be changed for the better because of it.

185. Prayer for growth

Please build up this church, Lord,
Not just in number
But in faith;
Not just in prosperity
But in hope;
Not just in influence
But in joy;
So that we might have a bigger impact on this
  community,
By your standards, not ours.

FOR MY TOWN, COUNTRY AND WORLD

186. For this nation

This is an amazing prayer when we think about the sort of country we live in, and our hopes for the sort of country it might be or become. Pray it, and then think about how you can join in with God's work in your nation to become part of the answer!

Almighty God, our Heavenly Father, bless our nation
that it may be a blessing to the world; grant that our
ideals and aspirations might line up with your will.
Keep us from hypocrisy in feeling or action.
Give us sound government and just laws, good
education and a clean press, simplicity and justice in
our relations with one another,

And, above all, give us all a spirit of service,
which will abolish pride of place and inequality of
opportunity.

Based on a traditional Anglican prayer

187. For godly government

Lord, let the government of my country look to you;
Would you turn their ears towards your word,
And their hearts towards yours,
In order that they would give leadership to this nation
That honours you, reflects your priorities, and brings
    you glory.

188. For our heads of state

God, bless the people at the very top,
And help them not to be filled with fear or pride,
Or to misuse the power they have been given.
May they be aware of you; may they look to you.
And through you may they learn to lead well.

189. For the big decisions

God be in the debating chambers and the corridors of
    power;
God be in the meetings and the conversations that
    matter;
God be in every part of the decision-making process,
And raise up men and women who will stand up for
    you within it.
Lord, save us from bad laws that dishonour you,
And place our country on a path that aligns more and
    more with your will.

190. For politics

Faith in politics and politicians has been eroded in the West in recent years, partly because of a feeling that some politicians are involved in governance because of the opportunity for profit through corruption. This old prayer demonstrates that these concerns are not new, and includes a wonderful rallying call for a new generation to get involved in politics, and act differently.

O God, great Governor of all the world,
We pray that you would strengthen justice and duty in
   our country's political life;
That the men and women who serve and represent us
   may feel ever more deeply that any diversion of their
   public powers for private ends is a betrayal of their
   country.
Raise up a new generation of citizens, who will have
   the faith and daring of the kingdom of God in their
   hearts,
And who will strive earnestly to maintain the freedom
   and rights of the people.

Based on a prayer by Walter Rauschenbusch (1861–1918)

191. For our environment

God, help me to take care of the planet you have
   entrusted to us,
Through big choices and through small,
In little lifestyle changes and in whole shifts of
   direction.
Guide my heart so that I know when something really
   matters,
And make me part of a generation that steps up and
   stands out on this issue.

But, Lord, I am only one person in a world of billions,
So I pray that you would move the hearts of people all
across it,
Whether leaders with the power to change laws
Or individuals with the opportunity to change their
lifestyle.
Prevent us, God, from killing your creation,
And hold its enduring beauty in your hands.

Amen.

192. For my home town

I lift to you in prayer the town where I live,
And ask that you would prosper it.
Make it a place where the streets are safe,
Where joy is more prevalent than sorrow,
And where your name is glorified.

Amen.

193. For these streets

Over these streets where I live, Lord, I pray your
protection;
That those who walk them would be safe from harm.

Amen.

194. For community

Lord, I pray that you would help those who live in this
place not to be simply a town, but a real community.
Teach us to love our neighbours; give us opportunities
to put one another first. May we know genuine

friendship; may we prize fairness and equality. And may those of us who know you so shine out your love so that those who live among and around us cannot fail to be drawn towards you.

Amen.

195. For all nations

God of all the nations, we ask for your help and
　your blessing.
Sustain in the people of this earth the spirit of justice
　and humility;
Enable us to recognize in other peoples and races their
　virtues, traditions, and rights.
Cultivate in us more fully the love of the arts of peace;
Purge our hearts of the suspicion of others,
And increase our confidence in one another;
That we may keep our place among the nations in
　peace and goodwill.

Based on a traditional Anglican prayer

196. Gone off course

Lord, lead this country back to you.
We've gone off course.
Shine out like a lighthouse to us,
And turn the ship around.

197. For a world that talks

Lord, we pray for the diplomats and the negotiators,
For the United Nations, for our own government,
For our allies, and for the rest of the world,

That the nations of this world,
From east to west and north to south,
Would continue to talk to each other
In the pursuit of peace and mutual understanding.
Lord, be in the rooms where conflicts can escalate
   and dissipate,
And by your Spirit build alliances even where they
   seem unlikely.

198. Prayer for the armed forces

Almighty God, you never sleep or slumber. Protect
and watch over all those who, at home or abroad, by
land, by sea, or in the air, are serving this country at
this time. We ask that they, being armed with your
defence, may be rescued in every moment of danger;
and, being filled with your wisdom and reinforced
with your strength, may do their duty, to your honour
and glory. Give them compassion and a desire to seek
justice in everything they do, and, as they are forced to
consider their mortality, give each man and woman an
awareness that you are by their side; that you are their
true commanding officer.

Amen.

Based on a traditional military prayer

199. Indiscriminate love

Spring up, Lord, in every corner of the world;
Break out in love, indiscriminately.
Evade logic; transform people and nations without
   warning.

Detonate joy in lands that have forgotten it.
Drive forward your kingdom, wherever and whenever
we least expect it.

200. International rescue

Lord, we pray for a revival in your church,
Not just at home, but in countries all around the
world.
From Asia to America, Lord, we would see whole
nations, continents even,
Turning to you as Saviour.
You, God, are the answer to six billion questions;
The response to every nation's prayers.
Though it blows our minds, we ask that you would
move in power,
Grab the attention of entire peoples,
Draw whole populations to yourself.
You can do it if you want to, Lord;
Send revival, that the whole world might know you.

FOR JUSTICE

201. Never close our hearts

Give us this day our daily bread, Father in heaven,
and grant that we who are filled with good things
from your open hand may never close our hearts to
the hungry, the homeless, and the poor; in the name of
the Father, and of the Son, and of the Holy Spirit.

From the Abbey of New Clairvaux, Viña, California

202. Justice-seeker's prayer

"The Lord is known by his acts of justice," says the
  psalm.
"He will never forget the needy;
The hope of the afflicted will never perish."

This is the God I follow,
Whose footsteps I walk in.
I want to be known as he is known,
As a seeker of justice;
As good news to the poor.
Help me, God, to live up to your name.

Based on Psalm 9:18

203. May the day come quickly

Father,
fill our hearts with deep compassion
for those who suffer,
and may the day come quickly
of your kingdom of justice and truth.

Amen.

Eugène Bersier (1831–89)

204. For the forgotten

Lord, to the forgotten,
The people who were born into countries and
  situations
Where resources are not rich, where the TV cameras
  do not journey,
I pray you would send such blessing that it would be
  beyond compare.

Strike joy into the hearts of the poor, and bring healing
to the sick,
And, as for me, make me someone who remembers
them,
In prayer and action, and all for your sake – you who
knows each of them by name.

205. For famine

In areas where there is famine, I pray that you would
send food and water;
But also, behind the scenes, where the greed of man
holds back aid,
I pray that you would move with such great force that
it would leave demons reeling.

206. Bread and justice

O God,
to those who have hunger, give bread,
and to us who have bread,
give the hunger for justice.

World Council of Churches

207. Prayer for the starving

Lord, I see on the television news images that I can't
believe, can't get my head around,
Showing that on this earth, where so many people
have more than they could ever need,
Children and their families are literally starving.
In a world where all-you-can-eat restaurants exist, that
cannot be fair;

In a world where the cost of the items in my bedroom
   could feed a family for a year, this isn't right.
Lord God, please send food for the hungry;
When they stretch their hands out today, please do not
   leave them empty.
And, Lord, please change the system.
Change governments. Change the heart of man.
Do not allow us to live in this way any longer.

208. For those who are suffering

Lord, help me today to see the world the way you do,
To look at those who are suffering
And be overwhelmed with compassion,
Driven to pray.
In the face of injustice and inequality,
Plant a desire in my heart
To help make a difference.
Help me to remember that prayer is powerful and
   changes things.
Although I am small, in you I am strong;
And although I feel powerless,
You stand next to me, and with you nothing is
   impossible.

Laura Haddow

209. Hearts and hands

Open our hearts and hands,
That we might reach out to the poor with your love,
And in doing so show them your face.

Amen.

210. Willing and ready

Lord, you were rich
yet, for our sakes, you became poor.
You promised in your gospel
that whatever is done
for the least of our brothers and sisters
is done for you.
Give us grace to be always willing and ready
to provide for the needs
of those whose parents have died
or whose homes are broken,
that your kingdom of service and love
may extend throughout the world,
to your unending glory.

St Augustine of Hippo (354–430)

211. Against corrupt governments

In those nations, Lord, where corruption holds up aid,
Where greed snuffs out hope,
We ask you to shake the systems
And cast out those who would do evil.
Would you take hold of those who would put their
   own profit before the health and safety of the poor,
And throw them out of power.
Topple corrupt governments, Lord;
Send your Spirit upon whistleblowers;
Fan the flames of uprising against oppressors.
Bring freedom to those enslaved by dictatorships,
And justice to the casualties of greed.

212. Halt the spread

Lord, halt the spread of HIV / AIDS
Worldwide, but especially in areas of poverty and
  pandemic,
Where communities are decimated, and drugs are out
  of reach.
Lord, bring miraculous healing, and step in by your
Spirit to prevent further infection.

Amen.

213. For a cure

Give skill, Lord, and divine inspiration,
To the scientists who search for an end to HIV.
Create a miracle, Lord; bless us with a cure,
And may the quest for profit have no say in its
  distribution.

214. Watch over the suffering

Watch, dear Lord,
with those who cannot sleep
and those who weep this night.
Tend the sick,
give rest to the weary,
and bless the dying.
Relieve those who are suffering,
have pity on those in great distress,
and shield those who are happy.

Amen.

St Augustine of Hippo (354–430)

215. For victims of trafficking

For the men, women and children caught up in the
    demonic trade of slavery I pray,
Asking you to break their chains and liberate them.
Stamp out trafficking through your people, Lord;
Give the legal systems of the world wisdom and
    expertise,
Give police in every nation a passion for justice,
And give us the spirit of Wilberforce: raise up a
    generation of abolitionists who will not stop
    until your kingdom obliterates the
    evil of slavery once again.

216. Cornerstone of peace

Almighty God,
the Great Thumb we cannot evade to tie any knot;
the roaring Thunder that splits mighty trees:
the all-seeing Lord up on high who sees even the
footprints of antelope on a rock mass here on earth.
You are the one who does not hesitate to respond to
    our call.
You are the cornerstone of peace.

African prayer for peace

217. For the voiceless

God, for those who have no voice
May we speak up,
And may you amplify us as we do,
So that they might be heard.

218. Justice here

Lord, I ask for justice not only in places that seem
   distant,
But also here where I live.
I pray for honest police and fair courts,
For laws that don't work in favour of the rich and
   the strong
And against the weak and the poor.
I ask that our politicians would be speakers of truth,
And that our churches would be filled with integrity.
Even if it hurts me, Lord, I pray that my life would
   speak of justice too,
That I might be in the centre of your will.

Amen.

219. To feel their needs

Lord, save us from being self-centred in our prayers
and teach us to remember to pray for others. May
we be so bound up in love with those for whom we
pray, that we may feel their needs as acutely as our
own, and intercede for them with sensitivity, with
understanding and with imagination.

John Calvin (1509–64)

220. Bring justice

God of justice,
Bring justice around me;
Bring justice through me;
Lead me by your Spirit to where it is not;
Empower me by your Spirit to make it so again.

FOR THE PERSECUTED CHURCH

In the West, we have the freedom to believe what we want, and sometimes that means we can take our faith and our God for granted. Yet in many parts of the church around the world, there is a huge cost attached to professing faith. Men and women are oppressed, imprisoned, tortured, and even killed for worshipping God, and, while incredibly these parts of the church are in many cases experiencing unlikely growth, they badly need our prayers. Here are just a few to get you started.

For more information on the persecuted church, visit: www.opendoors.org or www.csw.org.uk

221. For those in chains

For those in chains for their beliefs,
For those tortured because they cannot give up
    on you,
For those separated from loved ones because they are
    a part of your family,
We cry out to you, Lord.

For those who pay a heavy price for loving you,
For those marginalized because they prioritize you,
For those killed because you were more important to
    them than life itself,
We cry out to you, Lord.

Be close to the persecuted,
Closer even than the pain they suffer for your name;
Have mercy on them, and on those who oppress them,
And, somehow, work all these things for good.

Amen.

222. Put me in the place

Put me in the place of the persecuted;
Let me truly know what faith costs them;
Bind them to me, not as distant friends but as close
relatives,
And commit my life to praying for them,
Speaking out for them,
Never forgetting them.

223. Bless the persecuted

Jesus, you said, "Blessed are those who are persecuted because of righteousness, for theirs is the kingdom of heaven."* So, as we come to you in intercession for them, we ask that they would truly be blessed, and know the power of that blessing; that pain would cease; that hearts and spirits would not be broken, and that they would know the kingdom of heaven coming here, and now, to earth.

(*Matthew 5:10)

224. Growth against the odds

Where there is oppression and injustice in your
church, God,
I pray that you would ignite growth so fast and so
infectious
That faith spreads like wildfire, even against the odds.
Break the hearts of the captors and torturers, and turn
them impossibly to you;
Turn the ears of whole communities to hear the cries
of believers who suffer for your name,

And bring transformation so vast and so extraordinary
That governments and nations have no choice but to
    take notice of you.

225. Imagining my brother

I imagine my brother,
Holed up in solitary,
Living on bread and water,
Blinded by darkness,
Cold, sick, and alone except for you.

I picture my sister,
Taken from her home,
Beaten and tortured,
Dishonoured and disgraced,
Left with nothing except for you.

Lord of the persecuted, I stand with them and call
    to you.
Be close to my brother; reveal yourself to my sister.
Answer their prayers today;
May they know peace in you.

FOR PEACE

226. Peace, peace, peace

Holy God,
Lead me away from death and into life,
from falsehood to truth.
Lead me, Lord, from despair to hope,
from fear to trust.
Lead me, Lord, from hate to love,

from war to peace.
Let your peace fill our heart, our world, our universe.
Peace, peace, peace.

Adapted from a multi-faith prayer by Satish Kumar

227. For the peacemakers

Lord Jesus, we would answer your call to be
  peacemakers,
But we pray also for those men and women
For whom making peace is a full-time pursuit.
In areas of conflict, protect them as they stand in the
  gap between opposing forces;
In places of danger, send your angels to be beside
  them as they seek to defuse, disarm and restabilize.
In their darkest moments, Lord, shine a light
And allow them long life, that they might continue to
  pursue peace for all our sakes.

Amen.

228. Inter-faith prayer of peace

O God, you are the source of life and peace.
Praised be your name for ever.
We know it is you who turns our minds to thoughts
  of peace.
Hear our prayer in these days of crisis.
Your power changes hearts.

Muslims, Christians and Jews remember and affirm
that they are followers of the one God,
Children of Abraham, brothers and sisters;
enemies begin to speak to one another;

those who were estranged join hands in friendship;
nations seek the way of peace together.

Give to us:
Understanding that puts an end to strife,
Mercy that quenches hatred,
And forgiveness that overcomes vengeance.
Empower all people to live in your law of love.

Based on a prayer by Pax Christi

229. For harmony

Lord, in my community, my nation, and my world,
I ask you to foster harmony between people of
   different faiths,
That we would respect each other;
That we would even learn to love one another;
That we would not retreat into ghettos of faith and
   culture,
But live in peace together.

Amen.

230. Establish peace

All-powerful God,
Father of the whole of mankind,
Work in the hearts of the rulers of nations,
Turn the hearts of all the people of the earth,
Towards peace.
By the power of your Holy Spirit, establish peace
   among the nations,
On the foundations of all that is right,
Through Jesus, so that he – the Prince of Peace,
Might draw all nations to himself.

Based on a prayer by William Temple (1881–1944)

6

Relationships

As a teenage boy with unmanageable hair, an unhealthy obsession with the TV sci-fi series *Doctor Who*, and an unswerving refusal to put away my childhood Lego sets, two things were important to me. Friends first, girls second, and unifying them the vain hope that one day the two categories might cross over. For many years, they didn't. I don't think I was unique in that; as a youth worker, I have a pretty good idea that your friends are the most important thing in your world. And, as a human being, I'd guess it's pretty likely that you also spend a lot of time thinking about the opposite sex.

In the context of your life, then, this is a pretty important subject for prayer. Why pray about our relationships? First, because, since they're important to us, they're very important to God. The Bible tells us about several great friendships, David and Jonathan, and Ruth and her mother-in-law Naomi among them. Friendship is the bedrock of community, and God realizes its importance. Second, because no close relationship between two people has ever run without a hitch; we all have our flaws, and when we get close to each other there is always going to be some kind of tension somewhere along the line. And, third, because relationships can often increase temptation, whether that means the peer pressure created by two friends egging each other on in a dare, or the very natural temptations that arise when two people start to fall for each other romantically.

So this section cuts to the heart of your life now. If none of this is relevant to you, then you should probably check that you're still breathing. Use these prayers as a resource to bring the most important things in your life before God, and watch the health of your relationships improve as you do so.

SEX

231. Sex: help me

I don't always feel strong enough, God,
To go against the flow – to ignore all the other voices around me
Telling me sex is my right and my plaything.
Give me reserves of strength;
Lead me away from temptation,
And help me to think clearly at every moment.
As I try to honour you, support my every step;
Keep me from stumbling;
Catch me when I'm about to fall.
Help me to live a life of purity, each moment pleasing to you.

232. Boundaries

This could be a good prayer for a couple to say together, if they are making a commitment to sexual purity.

Give us boundaries that honour you, and keep us
   honourable;
Show us where the lines are, and help us to stay on the
   right side of them;
Increase our willpower in line with our affection.
As we enjoy each other, help us also to enjoy waiting,
And in those moments when we're in danger of
   forgetting ourselves,
We ask you to remind us of our promise to each other.

233. My vow

The world tells me that sex is my right,
That experimenting and "having fun" is normal and
   healthy.
Yet I am not a citizen of this world but of another,
And so I make a vow to you, Lord God:
To live in a way that flies in the face of culture,
To believe that I am worth more than it says I am,
To keep myself for marriage and for my God,
And, through doing so, to grow in you.

234. Questioning sexuality

This prayer is designed for someone who is struggling with or questioning their sexuality. It seeks to make no judgment – only to draw us closer to the God who loves us, whoever we are.

God of love, you know my struggle.
You know I have questions, that I feel different;

Help me to understand what it all means – help me to
truly know myself better;
Speak to me about who I am, and who you want me
to become.
Above all, Lord, I know that you love me completely,
without condition;
Your love for me is wider and higher and fuller than I
could possibly imagine.
As I think and pray and live through these questions,
Never allow me to forget the truth or the power of
your love for me.

235. Letter after a fall

*This prayer, written as a letter, is a heartfelt attempt to give words to
feelings of regret that may be experienced after we've made a mistake in
this area of our life.*

God,

I've messed up. I said I wanted to honour you with my
body, and I didn't live it out. I ask for your forgiveness
and your mercy, and for your help in dealing with
the fallout. But please don't allow me to be consumed
with guilt; please prevent others from pointing the
finger of blame. If it's possible, please give me a clean
slate; accept my regret and re-embrace me. Take
away this feeling deep in the pit of my stomach, and,
somehow, take this mistake and use it for good.

I'm so sorry. Please receive my prayer, and forgive me.

236. Under pressure

Lord, I long to live a life that pleases you
But it can be so hard not to give in to the pressures
   from those around me.
Help me to be so much stronger;
May my thoughts be fully in tune with yours.
Please help me to see sex as you designed it to be;
Not as a cheap, valueless thing to be shared with
   many
But as a beautiful and fantastic gift,
Something to be shared with one person, as part of
   being joined to them –
Joined not only in body, but also in a lifelong
   commitment –
And therefore joined to their heart and becoming a
   part of who they are.
Please bring that one person into my life one day.
Help me to resist the temptation to walk away from
   what I know to be true,
To give in, and go my own way.
Please guard my heart
And help me control my body and my thoughts.

Amen.

Laura Haddow

237. Porn prayer

The use of pornography is a huge issue, and one that most users are in denial about. If as Christians we are to think about "whatever is pure", we know that this isn't an area for us to be involved in. This prayer is a frank opportunity to be honest with God and seek his help if we are struggling with this matter. For more help, visit www.xxxchurch.com

Lord Jesus, I know that by your Spirit you are with me every moment of my life.

You know everything about me; you know my highs and my lows, my strengths and my weaknesses.

Since you know all this, you also know when I do things of which I am ashamed; you know the areas in which I struggle.

Lord, pornography has a hold on me – it is addictive and compulsive;

Though I tell myself it's harmless, I know that it is anything but.

Please, God, break the chains of this addiction;

Give me the strength to step away from this pattern of behaviour.

Put someone into my life to whom I can be accountable,

And lead me not into temptation as I try to live a porn-free life.

Lord, if damage has already been done to the way in which I view sex, relationships or myself, I pray that you would bring restoration.

For those involved in the creation of pornography I also pray, asking you to heal them of the unseen damage it has done to them, and giving them a way out.

And, Lord, in a world where porn has become a billion-dollar industry, I ask that you would move through rulers and legislators to break its power over so many.

238. Prayer for sexual addiction

Lord, I am consumed by sexual temptation, every
single day of my life.
Please take me firmly by the hand, and lead me away
from it,
That I might see people as more than objects,
And sex as the wonderful precious gift that you
intended it to be.

239. Against repression

I ask, Lord, that as I try not to fall into sexual sin
I would not by doing so become repressed.
Lord, give me a healthy view of sex and sexuality,
That, when the time is right, I might be able to
embrace it as you intended.
So keep me from thinking of sex as sin,
But rather lead me to the right person to share it with.

240. For preservation

Lord, help me to preserve my virginity,
That I might be free to share a wonderful gift on my
wedding night.

Amen.

BOYFRIEND/GIRLFRIEND RELATIONSHIPS

241. For a good relationship

Lord, you know the desire of my heart,
And that I'd really love to be in a relationship.
May it be your will that there's someone for me,

And not just anyone, but someone with whom I can
grow closer to you.
Someone who cares for me and puts me first;
Someone who listens as much as they speak;
Someone kind; someone honest.
Someone after your heart.
Please, Lord, draw me to someone like that.

Amen.

242. At the start of something new

I thank you for this new relationship, Lord, and ask
that you would be rooted at the centre of it, right from
the start. Then, wherever this goes, we will know
that we stand together on the firmest foundations. I
ask that your hand would be upon us both, so that
whether we are together or apart, we would honour
and glorify you. Show us how to love and respect each
other and, most of all, deepen our friendship. Lead us
on our journey together, Lord. Amen.

243. Centre us in you

Lord, bring our relationship back towards you;
Show us how to pray together without feeling
embarrassed,
To hold your word between us without any
awkwardness,
To remember you every time we are together,
And to treat each other in such a way that those who
know us cannot fail to be struck by the difference
in us.

244. For my relationship

Lord, bless this relationship with good times;
Season it with wisdom;
Fill it with selfless and unconditional love,
And surround it with yourself.

245. Prepare me

I pray, Lord, that my relationships now would be the
    right training ground for marriage in the future.
Protect me from making mistakes;
Through every relationship, teach me about myself
    and prepare me for the future,
So that, if you should lead me toward marriage, I
    would be mature enough to handle it,
Wise enough to succeed at it,
And loving enough to excel at it.

BREAK-UPS

246. Help me to break up

Lord God, you have walked with me all the way
    through this,
From our first meeting to the point when I knew it
    wasn't going to work.
I ask that you would give me wisdom as I explain that
    it's over;
That you'd be with me as I seek to make sense, be
    kind, and listen.
God, as I seek to finish this chapter well, please write
    the dialogue.

247. Restoration or closure

God, if it's right, if it's still possible for us to get back
together,
I ask that it would happen, and that I'd know your
hand at work.
Lord, if it's wrong, if it's time for this relationship
to end,
I pray that I would have closure, and a peace that
comes from you.

248. Broken-hearted

I feel utterly broken;
This news has hit me like a high-speed train.
It came out of nowhere – I didn't see it arriving, or at
least that's what I'm telling myself right now.
It's like I'm surrounded by the shattered pieces of my
heart;
Help me, God, to get my bearings again,
And to begin to put my life back together.
Keep me from making a fool of myself,
Rebounding,
Saying things I don't mean to anyone who'll listen.
Even as I feel like screaming, be the peace in my heart,
Lord,
And somehow get me through this.

249. Senselessness

Lord, I don't understand what has happened.
I thought it was going so well – I thought you were
right at the heart of it.
Please help me to make some sense of things.

Right now I feel like my life just blew up in my face.
Be in the midst of what's left.

250. Heal this wound

You know how long it's been, Lord.
You know I should be over this by now.
But every time I think about it, my stomach turns
inside me.
I don't know if I was in love, or if I just feel
desperately hurt;
All I know is that the feeling won't go away.
God who can heal the deepest hurts,
Please heal this wound inside me and make me
whole again.

FRIENDSHIPS

251. For those we love

Almighty God, we entrust all who are dear to us to
your never-failing care and love, for this life and the
life to come; knowing that you are doing for them
better things than we can desire or pray for; through
Jesus Christ our Lord. Amen.

Traditional Anglican prayer

252. For my friends

Thank you for the friends you've brought into my life,
For all the memories we share,
And for all the times we've had, both good and
difficult.

For the times we've laughed
And for the hard times
When we've been there for each other – supporting
and encouraging each other.

Help me to live out my faith and relationship with you
in a way that is real to them.
That in my small way I will be a faint reflection of who
you are;
That the decisions I make, places I go, and attitude
I have will make them see that there is something
different about me that comes from you.

Lord, I lift my friends to you.
You changed me in an amazing way and I know you
can change them too. Please plant faith in their
hearts and help them to come to know you.

Laura Haddow

253. For my best friend

Thank you, God, for my best friend,
For who you've made her,
The gifts and talents you've given her.
I pray that, wherever she is right now, you would
bless her;
Give her a special moment of joy that will brighten
her day.
Help me to be the best friend I can to her,
And reflect in our friendship the love and community
That exist in your Trinity.
Give us patience with one another, kindness and
gentleness;
May we learn from each other how to be more like
you.

Thank you for the gift of friendship;
Teach me every day to put my friends before myself.

254. No greater love

Jesus, you said:
"Greater love has no man than this: that he lay down
   his life for his friends."
You laid down your life for me;
Show me, in the big things and the small,
How I can live my life in a way that mirrors yours,
And lay it down daily for you and for others.

Amen.

255. Friends on a journey

Draw to me, Lord, friends who will understand me;
whose interests will complement mine; who know
you, and who will walk alongside me on this journey
of faith.

Give us, Lord, deep friendship, which isn't brittle, isn't
selfish, isn't competitive. Build in us a love for one
another, where each puts the other first.

Bind us, Lord, together, as we travel with you. As
companions on life's road, let us, by one another's
example, be changed more and more into reflections of
your Son.

256. For new friends

God, you know I love my friends,
But also that they can sometimes lead me astray.

While I would ask for willpower and self-discipline,
I am also aware that I need running mates in the race
   of faith.
The friends I have now are not yet that.
So I ask that you would bring me new friends to
   complement the old,
People who love you as I do, and who can help me to
   grow.
Lord, as I seek to stand against the flow for you, I feel I
   can't do it on my own;
Please, in your mercy, send others to stand alongside
   me.

257. My closest friends

Thank you for the people you've placed around me.
Help me to love and listen to them;
to bring out the best in them, and not the worst.

When my friends frustrate me, help me to be patient.
When my friends let me down, help me to forgive.

Help me to remember that you are my closest friend.

Helen Crawford

258. Lonely among friends

No one understands me;
No one listens;
No one really appreciates who I am inside.

Friends who used to be close are now far away,
But I miss the jokes, the support and the comfort of
   past friendships.

Please put people around me who will love and
  appreciate me,
and remind me that you are here, even when I feel
  alone.

259. Feeling friendless

Even though they tell me I'm being ridiculous,
I feel that my friends don't appreciate me.
I feel as if they don't really like me for who I am.
Lord Jesus, the closest friend I could ever have, I pray
  that you would make me wise,
That I would know if it's all in my head;
Gracious, so that even when my friends don't treat me
  well I would respond in love;
And strong, rooted in you so that even if I have not
  one friend on earth
I have a friendship with you that will endure for ever.

260. Comparing myself with friends

It's really easy to compare myself with others;
To feel worse than some people, and better than
  others.
But I am sure that this is not your way;
You made every one of us and you have no favourites.
Help me to see myself as you see me,
And to see others in the same light.

Helen Crawford

FRIENDS WHO DON'T KNOW YOU

261. Short prayer for a friend to come to faith

God, I ask that my friend _____
Would somehow, miraculously, through your
 intervention,
Come to know you.
This matters to me; I will ask you again and again.
Please work in his heart, and draw him to yourself.

262. Longer prayer for a friend to come to faith

Lord, you sent your Son to die for me,
For my family, for my friends.
Just as you died for me, you died for my friend _____.
I bring her name to you today,
Someone who does not yet know you personally,
And I ask that she would come to do so.
Work in the circumstances of her life, to point her
 towards you;
Give me the words, and refine my character, so that I
 might better reflect you to her.
Speak to her through any and every means;
Call her by name, and draw her to yourself.
I pray that she would know your voice and be brave
 enough to respond to it;
That even in a culture that rejects you, she'd be
 compelled to walk against the tide.
Bring her into a lifelong relationship with you, Lord,
That stretches into eternity.
Even more than that, I pray that her decision would
 cause shockwaves,

That one response to your love would bring two,
　　three, and more.
Bring all my friends to you, Lord,
But before you change even one,
I recognize that I need to change too –
So start with me.

263. Give me the words

Lord, please give me the words as I try, in my often
rambling and incoherent way, to tell my friends about
the incredible love that you have shown me. Help me
to make sense; when I'm asked big questions, please
speak through me; give me words that are not my
own. Help me to be honest and full of grace; give me
the strength not to dodge the challenge and present
only half of the message. Take this weak and flawed
vessel, Lord, and put me to work for your glory
among my friends. Amen.

264. Ripple effect

Lord, may your presence in me
Create a ripple effect that touches the hearts of all
　　my friends,
And, as time goes on, leads each and every one of
　　them towards you.

265. Persistent

I will ask you today that my friend would come to
　　know you,
And, if I see no progress, I will ask again tomorrow.
God, I will pray for my friend until you break into
　　their heart;

I will not stop until you do.
You have placed in me a love for them which means I
cannot give up.
Please, Lord, open their eyes to you today.
And, if not today, tomorrow.

FAMILY

266. For my family

Lord, help my family;
Help us to bear with each other,
To see one another through your eyes,
To think before we speak,
To never allow the love we have for each other to
become buried and assumed,
To grow together and to stay together.

267. For example

They're not perfect,
But, Lord, I thank you for my parents' example,
In loving me and each other.
Please continue to teach me about your love for me,
and about the love I should pass on,
In my own marriage and parenting and also in the
way I treat them.

268. Honouring them

Help me, God, to honour my father and mother,
And to know what that really means in every
situation.

Lord, there are so many things that they do that I find
difficult, or which annoy me.
So what does it mean to honour them?
Lord, I want to worship you through the way I treat
my parents – I ask that you would show me how
to do that, day by day.

Amen.

269. Brother, sister, daughter, son

In all the roles I play in my family, Lord,
I pray that you would show me how to play them
better.
As a child and as a sibling, as a cousin and more,
Help me to know what it is to be more like Jesus,
In every relationship I have,
In every role I play.
Let love pour out of me, Lord,
Let my family know that I am born again,
Not only because of the way I behave
But because of how I treat them.

270. A family that makes a difference

Lord, I pray that our family would make a difference
in this world;
That people would know our name; that they would
hear it and smile.
Give us a job to do, not just as individuals but as a
community bonded by blood;
Use us to transform the world around us;
Use us together, working shoulder to shoulder for
your glory.

FAMILY THAT DOESN'T KNOW GOD

271. The only Christian

Lord, it can be so hard to be the only Christian in
   my family.
I love them so much and thank you for them.
But since you came into my life
I know they've found it hard to understand who I am.
They know I've changed
But they don't realize that I've only changed because
   of you.

At times it can seem that they are just waiting for me
   to fail and fall back into being who I was;
Somehow waiting to catch me out.
Help me to be patient, knowing that you are helping
   me and that you know all about my life and the
   situations I face.
Help me to be strong
In conflicts and difficult situations;
To take a deep breath and seek your help before
   reacting in ways that are not honouring to you.
Help me to respect my parents,
Even when I can't agree with all the things they say;
To commit to praying for them daily,
As I try to share my faith with them.

272. I long for them to know you

I long for my family to know you too, Lord;
To know what it is to be yours.
Please help me to make my faith real to them,
And to have the right words to say when they ask me
   about you.

273. For a sibling

God, we grew up together,

Yet now it seems we're growing apart.

Please help my sibling to see that, in finding you, I've
not gone crazy;

That this isn't something that should divide us,

But bring us together.

Draw us both closer to each other, and to you, Lord.

Amen.

274. Alone at home

When it feels like I'm alone and no one understands,

Help me to remember that you are there in every
situation,

That you hear every difficult conversation,

And that you know the problems I face.

Though I often don't know how much to say, or what
words to use,

Please use me to bring my family to know you.

Strengthen my faith;

Help me to trust that with you nothing is impossible.

275. You are bigger

Even though my family say there is no God,

You are bigger than that.

Even though they tell me I've changed, that I've lost
my mind,

You are bigger than that.

Even though they say I'll grow out of it,

You are bigger than that.

Even though, if I'm honest, I find it hard to believe
they could ever become your followers too,

You are bigger than that.

School

You may think school is the last thing you want to pray for. I hope your schooldays are infinitely more rewarding and enjoyable than mine were. Academically unremarkable and, crucially, very bad at any form of sport, I was overlooked by my teachers and pushed around by my classmates. My schooldays are something I look back on with very little fondness, save for the time we locked one of the school bullies in the art-room kiln. (The day after that, when he had escaped alive, was less fun for me.)

Whether you love or hate your time at school, however, it might be that you don't often spend much time thinking about it when you come to pray. With the exception of one particular time of year, which we'll come on to, it's possible that you don't often seek God's help in your study, or pray much at all about the life of the school. Considering it's where you spend so much of your time, that might be a mistake.

The following collection of prayers is in two parts. The first takes the twenty-five most popular school subjects in the

UK (at the last count), and provides a simple prayer for each that seeks to involve God in your study of the subject. You may want to pray these once or occasionally, or even copy them into relevant notebooks.

The second section tackles the various parts of school life, from preparing for the exam period to – horror of horrors – praying for teachers! As you seek to live out your faith in the community of your school, I hope you find the prayers relevant and helpful.

SCHOOL SUBJECTS

276. English Literature

God who inspires poets,
Master storyteller, architect of life's great narrative,
Open my mind, that I may be inspired by literature;
Give me understanding, that I might see inside the
    story,
And show me where your hand can be traced
In the foreground and in the subtext of great writing.
Give me appreciation of poetry and prose,
And help me as I work to critique and analyse it.

Amen.

277. English Language

Thank you, Lord, for language – for the nuances and
    intricacies that make it spectacular,
For metaphor, rhyme and rich vocabulary.
Assist me as I seek to understand its complexities;
Help me to get the rules straight in my head,
And, in every way, help me always to use language
    well.

278. Maths

As I look at the numbers,
Be in the midst of them, God;
As I calculate, keep my mind focused, sharp and fresh.
You are Lord of all – even of number, formula and
    shape.
Help me to understand and to learn,
And, in my head as well as on the page,
May it all add up.

279. Science

God, you are the creator of everything we call science;
Give me insight into the workings of your creation;
And teach me how my faith intersects with the
    theories and the claims of the textbook,
So that I may see your hand at work in every new
    thing that I learn.

280. Chemistry

You created the elements, formed them out of nothing;
You placed everything in intricate balance,
Painted a million-colour canvas and called it the
    universe.
Help me to understand these building blocks of
    existence;
Give me boldness and wisdom as I experiment with
    them,
And remind me that you are the great scientist behind
    it all.

281. Biology

God, help me in the study of biology;
There is nothing that lives into which you did not
   place life –
All of it rests in your hands.
Inspire and enrapture me with the incredible works of
   your hands,
And help me to understand how things are, and how
   they have come to be.

282. Physics

Help me to understand how the universe behaves,
And never to forget that you underpin it.
Simplify the complexities so that my mind can grasp
   them;
Illuminate my study and grant me a passion for my
   subject;
And give me an insight into the way things work,
That, through seeing into the engine of the world you
   created, I might know you better.

283. Geography

God of the whole world,
You chose not to place us in an arid landscape,
   but into an incredible creation.
Reveal more of it to me each time I come to study,
And renew my appreciation over and over again for
   the beauty and the wonder of the world you have
   made.

284. History

As I look into the past, help me to join the dots
Between your grand story,
The story of man,
And the story you are writing in me.

285. RE

As I study faith in all its forms,
May I be respectful, open-hearted, honest and true to
what I believe.
Through it all, may I draw closer to you,
And, in doing so, draw others towards you too.

286. ICT

You are an ancient God; you are an eternal God.
You were in the creation of technology; in the same
way you know its future.
Help me to harness the opportunities that machines
create,
To understand them fully, and to be wise about their
limits.

287. Design and Technology

As I study design, Lord,
Give me a fraction of your aesthetic eye,
A minuscule portion of your creative flair,
And a tiny part of your insight into how materials
behave,
So that I might be able to understand how things
work,
And, through my creativity, bring worship to you.

288. Music

In the beauty of music, your presence is felt;
Through the study of the art, may I know you ever
   more deeply.
Even in the classroom or in practice,
Overtake me with the creativity of your Spirit;
Increase my gifts in reading, playing, writing,
   comprehending;
And give me every opportunity to worship you
   through music.

289. Psychology

As I seek to understand the mind and human
   behaviour,
Give me your eyes to perceive, your wisdom to
   understand,
And your discernment to know what is going on in
   every case.
Through study and application, I pray you would
   increase my skills and gifts,
And use me to help others, now and in the future.

Amen.

290. Media Studies

As I study a world of communication and creativity,
   God,
Help me to be a sharp analyst,
An eloquent speaker,
A critical consumer,
And a perceptive thinker.

Lead me to walk in purity and with discernment,
And enable me to create media of substance that
honour you.

291. Business

I want to learn about business,
But I also want to keep ambition and finance in
  perspective.
Prosper my understanding, Lord,
But do not let me sacrifice myself to false prosperity.
Give me a head for business,
That I may put it to work for you.

292. Art and Design

Artisan God, you have inspired masters;
Now you inspire me.
Be the X-factor in my work,
The spark of divine genius.

293. Drama/Theatre

Thank you, God, for the gift of theatre,
For the joy of observing and enacting drama,
For masterful writing,
For the spine-tingling excitement of improvisation.
Lord, as I study a source of enjoyment,
Please protect my love of it; do not let me run dry;
Instead, encourage me to throw myself in, over and
  over again at the deep end,
And use every dramatic gift you've given me for
  your glory.

294. Politics

Give me a passion to make a difference,
A heart for justice,
A sense of right and wrong,
A level head and a listening ear,
An ability to make my point,
And a knowledge of how to bring change.
May my heart always be soft, and my mind open to
the idea that I might be wrong.
Above all, may I be a force for good, for you;
In the classroom, in debate, and beyond.

295. PE/Sports Science

You have given us bodies that can do extraordinary
things;
And when we run we can feel your pleasure.
Through sport, may I worship you;
May I experience joy and greater health,
And learn to help others to know the same.

296. Law

God of justice,
Make me exceptional in the field of law;
Optimize my mind for the task,
So that in my life I might be good news to those who
seek justice.

297. French

Seigneur Dieu,
Aide-moi à mieux comprendre cette langue,
A parler plus clairement,

A parfaire ma lecture et mon écriture,
Afin qu'elle devienne un outil que je puisse garder
   tout le reste de ma vie,
Et qui soit utile entre tes mains.

298. German

Unser Herr Gott,
Hilf mir bitte, diese Sprache besser zu verstehen,
Und klarer zu sprechen,
Und mein Lesen und Schreiben immer mehr zu
   verbessern,
Damit es ein Geschick sei, das ich lebenslang
   aufrechterhalten kann,
Um es für deine Zwecke zu benutzen.

299. Spanish

Señor Dios:
Ayúdame a comprender mejor este idioma,
A que pueda hablarlo con mayor claridad.
Que mi forma de leerlo y escribirlo se perfeccionen
   continuamente,
Para que conserve esta capacidad durante el resto de
   mi vida,
Y pueda utilizarla provecho contigo.

Lord God,
Help me to understand this language better,
To speak more clearly,
To refine again and again my reading and my writing,
So that this might be a skill that I can keep for the rest
   of my life,
And put to use for you.

300. Languages

Help me to embrace language beyond my own,
Even when it does not come naturally;
God, stretch me and grow me through the processes of
  speaking, listening, reading, and writing,
And assist me in learning and understanding,
So that I might be equipped with skills that increase
  the horizons of my life.

THE EXAM PERIOD

301. Revision prayer

Help me, God, as I come to revise:
Keep my mind fresh and my appetite strong,
Bless me with memory and with understanding;
Give me the discipline to put the time in,
And reward me for my hard work.
I pray that as I look back over everything I have
  learned
It would make sense,
That you would join the dots in my head,
That I would give a good account of myself,
And so prepare fully for the challenge of exams ahead.

302. Each exam fresh

Help me, God, to face each exam fresh,
My mind uncluttered from the one before.
If others have gone well, may I not be overconfident;
If they have been difficult, may I not dwell on them.
Keep my eyes only on the paper in front of me,

And fill my memory with the fruit of my revision.
Help me to give myself the best chance of success
In every exam I take.

303. Against stress

In this exam period, Lord,
Keep me focused, but keep me relaxed;
Do not let me become stressed.
Please protect my sleep, and give me unbroken rest,
And send me into each exam room with the right kind
   of energy.

304. Procrastinating

Lord, save me from the art of doing nothing;
Distract me from distraction;
Focus me on what's important.
Keep me from doodling;
Unplug me from social networking;
Turn my eyes back to the books.
May the phone not ring;
May the doorbell stay silent.
I want to revise; God, help my natural aversion to it!

305. When I'm distracted

Refocus my attention;
Remove distraction.
Centre me in you;
Bring me back to my studies again.

306. Be in my revision

Lord, at this time of revision
With so much to do
And with exams not far away,
I pray for focus and concentration.
As I sit here
I can find myself getting so easily distracted
And drawn away by other things that fight for my
    attention.
Please shut those voices off,
And give me focus for the things I need to do.
I pray for a real sense of peace and stillness that will
    overcome any restlessness and nerves;
I lift this entire time of revision to you.
Please help me to have good, restful nights of sleep
Where my brain and body can be recharged and
    refreshed,
And after which I'll be ready to start each day awake
    and alert.
I pray for help in remembering the things I need to;
Thank you, Lord, that you care about every part of
    my life.

Laura Haddow

307. Exams approaching

Help me to keep things in perspective
and not to worry about the exams
or to care too little.

When pressure overwhelms me,
remind me that you hold my future in your hands,
and that all does not rest on the result of this study.

Help me to manage my time well,
to make time to rest and play
as well as study.

Help me to revise effectively,
and to remember all that I have studied during the
exam.
May I always give you all the glory for all that I am
and do.

Helen Crawford

308. Motivation

God, when my motivation is low,
Inspire me;
And help me to enjoy the work that I do.
When I just can't get myself going,
May I see my hard work as an act of worship to you.

309. In the room

Lord, when I am in that room, where the ticking clock
punctuates the silence, where I know that every stroke
of my pen can help to define my future, I pray that I
will know your presence there too. Come as close to
me as my own breathing; calm my heart and galvanize
my mind. Relieve any sense of pressure, and bring to
the front of my memory everything that I have studied
and now need to recall. Be with me, Lord God, in this
defining moment. Amen.

310. On an exam day

Thank you that, whatever the outcome today,
I know you have a plan for my life.
Please take my achievements and failures
And weave them into something amazing for you.
I hope for success today, but, much more than that,
My desire is to become the person you want me to be.

PRAYING FOR YOUR SCHOOL

311. For my teachers

Thank you, God, for the teachers at my school, and
    especially those who teach me;
Even though I sometimes find them difficult to like,
I pray you would bless each one of them today.
For each department I thank you,
For every man and woman who has chosen to educate
    us for a living, I am grateful.
Bless this school and most of all its staff;
Today, may they know the peace that comes from you
Rather than the frustration that must often come from
    teaching us!

312. For Christian teachers

I thank you for the men and women who teach here,
    and who know and love you;
Lord, they have to walk a difficult line, especially
    when it comes to sharing their faith.
I pray you would give them opportunities to talk
    about you that don't put their job in danger;

That they would be able to influence the direction of
the school for you;
That they would know you close by throughout every
working day,
And that they might support each other in their faith
and their work.

313. For my Christian Union

Through a few voices, you can make a big impact,
Lord;
With a few willing souls, you can start a revolution.
God, I ask you to bless our Christian Union
With courage, vision, integrity, and joy.
Fill our meeting places with your love, Lord,
That we might be like the carriers of a virus,
Which spreads across this whole school.

314. A school that brings you glory

Almighty God, in whom we live and move and have
our being,
Make this school like a field which the Lord has
blessed,
So that purity, truth, kindness and justice flourish here.
Give us a good name and reputation,
Make us useful to our wider community,
And use all of us as instruments of your glory,
For the sake of Jesus Christ our Lord. Amen.

Based on a prayer by Henry Hayman (1823–1904)

315. For the head teacher

Lord, I lift to you the head teacher of my school,
And ask that you would give him wisdom, integrity,
  and sound judgment.
I pray that he would know you as Saviour,
But even if not,
Let your hand always be on his shoulder,
Guiding him in justice, in mercy, in his priorities.
I pray you would teach him to manage his staff
So that they don't burn out but flourish,
And help him to feel liked and respected,
Even through the alienating boundaries of his job.
Finally, I pray that he would have a life outside school,
And that he would have balance between work and
  the world beyond it.
Please bless our head teacher today, Lord God,
And teach us all to respect him better.

Amen.

SCHOOL LIFE

316. When I don't agree

Though I know you want me to respect my teachers,
You don't always call me to agree with them.
If their words conflict with yours, Lord,
Give me the discernment to realize it.
Give me the wisdom and grace to respond;
Show me when it's time to turn away,
And when it's time to stand up and speak out for you.

317. Deadlines

Give me the gift of meeting deadlines, Lord,
So that I can build a good reputation for myself,
And honour you in the process.
Heal me of any last-minute tendencies,
And help me to find joy in handing things in on time.

318. Distinctive

May I be distinctive in my school; stand out from the
crowd for you.
May people see the difference in me, and know that
you are responsible for it.
May my classmates ask questions of me, and may I
have good answers.
May everything I do at school and at home reflect well
on you,
And may others be drawn towards your light as a
result.

319. I would radiate you

Heavenly Father,
As someone who belongs to you,
Help me to radiate you in the way I live my life;
Especially at school, where I spend so much of my
time each week,
I pray for your help in living out my faith.
As I spend time alongside so many who don't know
you,
Help me to understand what it means to be a good
witness to the things you've done in my life,
In my attitude to others,

In the way I behave,
In the respect I show for those around me.
Help me to be a voice for peace in squabbles and
  disagreements,
To draw alongside those who are struggling or alone,
And to be a friend even to those I wouldn't naturally
  choose to be friends with.
Help people to notice there is something different
  about me
And that the difference is you.

Amen.

320. This class

Help me to love my classmates, as you do;
To see them through your eyes –
Even the ones I don't get on with,
Even the ones that clearly don't like me.
Allow me to think bigger than that,
And to put their needs and problems before my own.

PROBLEMS AT SCHOOL

321. Punishment prayer

A prayer for when you've been punished at school.

Lord, help me to receive this punishment
Without being smart, without feeling resentment.
Help me to learn and grow through being disciplined,
And help me not to speak badly of my teachers as a
  result.
May my response to just punishment be a kind of
  worship to you.

322. Bullied

This prayer is for someone who is being bullied at school. If that's you, this prayer may not sum up how you're feeling, but hopefully it can be adapted. Be assured: God always hears us when we cry out to him.

> I pray, Lord God, that you might intervene when the
> bullies come for me.
> Distract them, interrupt them;
> Much more, I ask that you would work in their hearts,
> So that they might grow up
> And leave me and others alone.
> I don't understand why they pick on me,
> But I don't know how to make it stop either.
> Please hear my cry, God;
> Step in. Protect me. Give me hope.
>
> Amen.

323. Stand guard

> God, rescue me from those at my school who would
> wish me harm.
> Stand guard over me, protect me, strengthen me, and
> save me.

324. Wishing for the weekend

> Isn't school supposed to be easier than this?
> Each morning I wake up wishing it was the weekend;
> My days are full of discomfort.
> So, Lord God, I ask you to change my mind,
> To give me a new perspective on school,
> To work on my behalf in some of the things I find
> hard.
> For me to enjoy school would be a miracle,
> But I'm willing to ask you to make it so.

325. Struggling

You know, Lord, that I'm struggling at school,
That I'm not finding the work easy.
I ask that you would give me the mental strength to
  apply myself,
The concentration and the focus to think clearly.
Draw near to me, Lord; support and encourage me,
And help me to get through this.

Amen.

Life

Growing through any stage of life has its fair share of complexities and pressures, but the teenage years are perhaps the most complicated of all. As the restrictions of childhood begin to fade away, the opportunities to choose your own path seem to increase in every area of life. Alcohol and other drugs appear on the horizon; money becomes a much more important (and seemingly scarce) commodity. We are forced to make moral and ethical decisions every day that could shape the course of the rest of our life. In our teenage years, we begin to decide who we are.

As Christians, it is also the point for many of us where we start to ask God who he wants us to become, and prayer therefore becomes a vital tool. The prayers in this short section cover ground ranging from our use of possessions to our engagement with politics, to our choices about work and university. Use them, and then use your own words to ask God for his help and guidance through this incredible but also challenging period of your life.

ALCOHOL AND OTHER DRUGS

326. Trapped

God, I feel totally trapped,
Swallowed up and entombed by this addiction.
Throw me a rope,
And give me the strength to hoist myself out of this.

327. Lord, I'm struggling

Lord,
I'm struggling…
So many friends in my life are getting involved in
    taking drugs and drinking,
And I'm finding it hard to fight the temptation to do
    the same.

I know it's wrong,
But it's so hard to stand out as being different,
Especially when it feels like I'm the only one.

And as I find myself in places where I know I
    shouldn't be,
I'm torn between what I know is right
And the lure of fitting in with the crowd.

I don't want to lose my friends through this
But I don't want to damage my body either,
Or choose to do things that will lead me away
    from you.

I know that getting involved in these things will cloud
    my decisions, thoughts and judgments,
And take me into situations that are not good for me.

Help me to remember that the Holy Spirit lives in me
And where I go, you go too.

I know I don't fight these battles alone;
Help me to be strong, a good witness to my friends.
Lord, I long to see them turn to you.

Help me to be brave enough to live distinctively
As a light in a dark room,
To be ready to share my faith
And to see my friendships as your mission field
   for me.

I pray for wisdom and strength.
Lord, help me live for you every day.

Laura Haddow

328. Knowing the difference

May I know the difference, God,
Between one drink and ten,
Between legal and illegal,
Between enjoyment and abuse.
May I know where the lines are,
And, with your help, stay on the right side of them.

329. No hold

Lord, may alcohol have no hold over me;
No power to dominate and undermine me.
Give me the right perspective on drinking,
And save me from letting myself down.

330. "Casual" drugs

When casual drug use is happening around me,
Lord, give me the strength not to be casual about it.
You have given me principles and I want to stick to
    them;
I know that taking drugs is not your best for me;
Help me to stand up for what I believe in with reason
    and with grace,
And, instead of following the herd, may I encourage
    others to change.

MONEY AND POSSESSIONS

331. Financial perspective

Jesus, you said that the love of money is the root of all
    kinds of evil;
I pray then that I would neither love money nor
    serve it,
But instead have your perspective on it,
And learn how to use it for you.

332. Keep me out of debt

Though the world around me is drowning in debt,
And full of people desperate to give me credit,
I pray that you would protect me from the choking
    debt
That has engulfed this culture.
May I learn to be content with what I have,
May I be wise with the resources you have allowed
    me,

And may I always know the difference between the
things I want and the things I need.

333. Neither poverty nor riches

Father,
Help me to remember that all things come from you.
When I long for things I can't afford, help me to
remember that "a man's life does not consist in the
abundance of his possessions".
Please provide the things I need and help me to be
content with what I have.
Teach me, like the author of Proverbs, to say:
"Give me neither poverty nor riches,
but give me only my daily bread.
Otherwise, I may have too much and disown you
and say, 'Who is the Lord?'
Or I may become poor and steal,
and so dishonour the name of my God."

Helen Crawford (based on Proverbs 30)

334. I am not

I am not just the sum of my possessions.
I am not just a consumer.
I am not just here to earn money.
I am not just here to buy stuff.
I am here because the King of Kings put me here,
For a purpose far beyond earning or spending or
gambling or accumulating.
I am here to love, and to pursue things that money
cannot buy.

335. Rejecting consumerism

I want to stand against consumerism;
I don't want my life to be defined by what I buy,
Or to make my decisions based on what feels good
    for me.
Help me to commit to good things even when they
    don't "pay off",
And to invest in things that don't earn me anything.

I want to stand against individualism;
I no longer live for myself;
Instead, I live for you and for the people you've put
    around me.
Help me to put myself last,
And live instead with community in my heart.

ETHICS AND CHOICES

336. Grow my respect

Lord, I'm part of a generation that kicks back against
    authority
– sometimes with good reason –
But, as for me, I want to honour you in all that I do.
So deprogramme any part of me that has been
captivated by unrighteous anger;
Grow my respect for the laws of my land,
And show me how to challenge them where challenge
    is needed.

337. Use my gifts

God,
Thanks for making me as you have.
Help me to discover the gifts you've planted in me.
Inspire me to invest in them.
Help me to enjoy what I turn my hand to,
And to work at everything as if I'm doing it for you.
May I reflect you in all that I do, and
Use all that I am for your glory.

Helen Crawford

338. When to stand up

Lord, help me to know when to stand up and be
   counted,
And when to sit down and be quiet.
May I know the difference between the fevered
   prompting of my ego,
And the still, small voice of God, nudging me to
   action.

339. Decision wisdom

God, be in my decision-making.
As I make choices each day between right and wrong,
   be my guide.
Give me a mind that thinks like yours,
And a heart that follows yours,
So that as I make my choices in life, liberated by the
   freedom you have given me,
I do not desert the walk of faith to which I've
   committed myself.

340. Questioning abortion

I hope that this prayer will never be relevant to you. If it is, and you are facing the question of whether to have an abortion, then please use it among your own prayers, and as part of your decision-making process. The words do not seek to make a judgment, but simply to reach out to God when you might feel embarrassed or ashamed to do so.

Lord, I know you love me, whatever I do;
The fact that I'm in this situation makes zero
   difference to your love for me.
I'm pregnant, and I wish I wasn't;
I didn't plan this, and I'm scared that whatever I do
   next will define my future.
I pray that you would speak to me clearly;
Give me an answer and a peace along with it.
Put good people around me who will help without
   making judgments,
And continue to walk with me as I deal with the
   consequences of my decision, all the days of my life.
I love you and I'm sorry.
I receive your forgiveness, and your overwhelming
   love for me,
Which hasn't diminished since the day I was born.
Please take me by the hand, Lord;
Please show me what to do.

THE FUTURE

341. Use me to make a difference

Heavenly Father,
I pray that although I am just one
You will use me to make a difference.
In whatever the future holds for me,
In the places you will take me,
The things I will do for you,
The life I will lead,
I pray I will walk each step with you.
I look forward to the adventures you will take me on,
The challenges you will give me,
Especially the ones I feel are impossible
But with your help I can attempt.
Thank you that, although these paths are hidden
    from me,
You know.
Help me to be open to your leading
And ready to follow where you call me to go.

Laura Haddow

342. Lead me wherever

God, though the road ahead seems uncertain,
I know you hold my future in the palm of your hand.
Help me not to be anxious, but teach me instead to
    lean into you,
To look to you for guidance when the choices are
    many,
To trust in your plan when I seem to be going off
    course.

As I make the big decisions, give me your wisdom, Lord,
And lead me wherever you want me to go.

343. Journey to adulthood

God, I want to live my whole life with you;
I undertake that when I put away the things of my youth,
My faith will not be one of them.
I want to know you at every age and stage of my life,
To feel your presence by my side in every hour.
As I draw near to you, Lord, please draw near to me;
Do not let my foot slip on the journey to adulthood.

344. Transition into work

Lord, as I enter the working world
I pray that I would feel you closer than ever;
That you would calm my nerves and focus my mind.
Help me to concentrate, to avoid simple mistakes;
Make me a team player, always having time for the people I work with.

I pray too that my faith would mark me out as a diligent and hard worker,
That my employers and colleagues would know me as a person of integrity,
And that everyone I encounter would see the difference that you make in me,
Be drawn to you through me,
And in meeting you be transformed.

345. Transition into university

My whole life is about to change;
The doorway to freedom is gaping open.
Give me, Lord, the maturity I need at this time.

My horizons are exploding;
A world of competing ideas hits me from every angle.
Give me, Lord, the resilient, intelligent faith I need to
  endure.

My choices are many;
I can choose to be whoever I want from this point on.
Give me the courage to become the person you made
  me to be.

346. Freshers' week prayer

Lord, in this week of opportunity and temptation,
Please hold on tightly to me.
Place people around me who love you and care
  for me;
Give me sober judgment even if I've had a few drinks;
Help me not to make mistakes that will define my
  future here;
Keep me immovably rooted in you.

347. For my gap year

I give you this year, Lord God, and ask you to hold
me so tightly as we journey through it together. May
no moment be wasted; may every day teach me
something new about you, and about myself. Make
it transformational: change my heart and refine my
character. Lord, this year is yours – do with it what
you will.

348. For university finance

Education is so expensive;
Please, God, find me a way
To extend my learning
Without crippling myself or my family with debt.

349. A right attitude

Lord, as I continue my life after school,
Give me a right attitude in everything I do.
Pour out your refining fire on my heart and my
    character;
Make me into the person I've always hoped to be
    for you,
So that, in this new stage of life, I would no longer be
    bound by the expectations of those who know me,
But plot a new course for myself,
Steering clear of unwise and unhelpful things,
And sailing into the plans and purposes that you've
    laid out for me.

350. Moving to a new place

God, though I've moved to a new town,
I have not moved away from you.
You were always here, just like you were always there;
I cannot run from you, nor would I want to.
In this new place, I pray you would help me to find:
New friends, who share my heart;
A new church, which can support me, and where I
    can invest;
And new places and ways to worship you through
    enjoying the gifts you've given me.

Let me not forget the place I have come from,
But here may I reach my full potential in you.

Praying through
the story

The Bible: dusty old fairy tale, or handbook for life? Well, probably neither, actually. The Bible is a huge story involving real people and real places; much of the content is backed up by the findings of historical scholars – so it's no fairy tale. On the other hand, if we approach it simply as a reference book on how to live, we're going to be disappointed, and miss out on much of what it has to offer. Instead of seeing it as some kind of manual with straightforward answers to tough questions, we need to appreciate that it is, in some miraculous way that we don't understand, a living book. I don't just mean that the stories of people following God thousands of years ago can also be applied to us today – I mean that the story is *alive*. When you are reading the Bible, it has the power to speak to you in a completely individual way. No one in history has ever been you before, reading the book through your eyes, in the midst of the life that you uniquely are living. The Bible can speak into that life, into that situation you're facing.

Put simply, the words of the Bible are often the clearest method through which God can speak to us. If you think that verse you just heard was scarily relevant to your life, it wasn't a coincidence – that may well have been God speaking. Of course the Bible contains answers – the gospels all contain a clear explanation of the meaning of life – but, to really understand it, we need to get to grips with *all of it*, by which I mean we need to see the big picture of the grand biblical story. When we understand the big themes and the overarching story of the Book, we start to see much more clearly where we fit into that story.

This section, then, takes a twenty-five-step journey through that big story. Each step contains a short Bible reading and two prayers: the first a prayer of thanks and praise for the truth of the story and an engagement with the subject; the second a personal response to it. Use these resources however you like, but see this as an opportunity to – in prayer – understand God's story just a little better.

Note to youth leaders: The twenty-five "steps" taken through the biblical narrative here are mirrored by meeting guides in my book The Ideas Factory *(also published by Monarch). These contain discussion-starters and questions to work through with youth in a range of settings.*

(I) CREATION

Read: Genesis 1

351.

> Creator God, you are an inexhaustible fountain of
> creativity;
> Your hands are those of the great artist, the master
> craftsman.

You spoke the universe into being – put the stars into
their places,
Separated darkness and light, land from sea.
What you did at the point of creation is inconceivable;
We cannot understand it, and yet we see the evidence
of it,
So we worship you.
God, you filled the earth with beauty, colour and
difference;
You did not stop until it was very good – even by your
standards!
And then you made us – the pinnacle of all you'd
made;
You lavished your creative flair upon us.
Creator God, we worship you.

352.

When I was a small child, the world filled me with
awe and wonder.
Now I walk past mountains without glancing up.
Recreate in me, God, that sense of wonder,
That I might not be so busy with the ugly necessities
of life
That I overlook the beauty right in front of me.

(II) SIN

Read: Genesis 3

353.

God, we are a fallen people;
Thank you, God, that you do not give up on us.

Even though our sin recurs like a broken record,
Your love persists.

354.

I am sorry, God, for when I step into the place of
    Adam and Eve,
When I choose my own way instead of yours;
When I listen to the voice of temptation instead of
doing what I know is right;
When I disregard the things I know you have said
    to me.
For every time I trip, mess up, and reoffend,
God, I ask your forgiveness.
Lead me not into temptation,
But deliver me from evil.

Amen.

(III) GOD'S PEOPLE

Read: Genesis 15

355.

Thank you, God, for your promise to Abram;
For establishing a people on earth when you might
    have given up on us.
Thank you that you chose to use flawed humanity to
    accomplish your plans,
When you could so easily have done it all without us.
Thank you that you still choose to use us today –
That your story goes on,

That it lives in human flesh.
Thank you, God, that you call us your people.
What an honour to be the people of the Living God!

356.

As I step into the great story that you've been spinning
    for millennia,
Give me a sense, Lord, of my place in it.
Show me an insight into your plans,
And thrust me into the middle of them.

(IV) GOD HEARS THE CRY

Read: Exodus 3

357.

We praise you, God, because you are not absent;
You do not keep yourself removed, turning your ear
    away from us.
Instead you engage, you involve yourself in human
    history;
When we cry out, you hear us.
Thank you, God, that you hear the cry,
Just as you did when Israel was enslaved.
More than that – you act, you intervene;
We worship you, God, because you care enough to
    come after us,
To rescue us when all our hope is lost.

358.

> Lord, I cry out to you –
> You know my struggles;
> You know how insurmountable they seem.
> Hear my cry, God of Moses;
> Deliver me from the evil that I face;
> Liberate me from the things that enslave me.

(V) THE LAW

Read: Leviticus 14:2

359.

> Thank you, God, that you care so much about us;
> you're interested in the tiniest parts of our lives.
> Thank you that you gave your people a law, a code of
> morality that would see them through life. Thank you
> that, despite their sin, you gave them a way to remain
> close to you. Thank you that, through Jesus, that's just
> as true today as in the time of Moses. Amen.

360.

> Despite everything you are,
> You still draw close to me.
> Despite everything I am,
> You still draw close to me.
> Thank you, God.

(VI) GOD'S SUPREME POWER

Read: Joshua 6

361.

God of the miraculous,
We thank you for the story of Jericho,
Where the impossible was made possible.
We praise you because of your extraordinary power;
You reign supreme over all the earth – you could wipe
  us from it in a heartbeat.
Yet you choose to put your power to work in us;
Your power goes with your people.

362.

You know my Jericho;
I believe that as Joshua stood outside that city,
And as I stand in opposition to the problems in my
  life,
The same God who was by Joshua's side is now by
  mine.
Lord, help me to overcome;
Teach me to trust you – to put my hope in you.
And, Lord, even in the most impossible situation,
Bring down the walls.

(VII) ISRAEL'S GREATEST KING

Read: 2 Samuel 9

363.

Thank you, Lord, for the story and example of King David,

For a hero of our faith from whom we have so much to learn.

In spite of his weaknesses, thank you for the man he was –

That he loved you, and sought after your heart,

That he led with integrity, and had compassion on the weak.

Thank you that, though he was a great king and warrior, he loved you first,

And that he loved you through the way he loved his people, your people.

364.

Give me a character like David's, Lord;

Place in me a concern for the poor and a heart for the oppressed;

Where I lead, let me lead with honour;

When I gain glory, let me turn it over to you.

Grow in me a heart that searches for a connection with yours,

A heart that puts you first.

I pray that I would always understand my place in the world as your child,

And continually run back to my Father, as David did.

May my transformed character be the clearest sign to others

That you live in me, because you *are* alive.

(VIII) GOD SPEAKS THROUGH HIS PROPHETS

Read: 1 Kings 18

365.

There is no God but you, Lord;
You are the one and only, unrepeatable, all-powerful God.
Though you are majestic,
You get your hands dirty;
You watch over us, listen to us, speak to us.
Thank you, God, for your prophets, today and yesterday;
That even though you are in every sense awesome,
You choose to speak through people;
And that as you spoke through Elijah and backed him up with your power,
You speak to us still today, and your power has not waned.

366.

Speak to me, God,
And give me the discernment to hear you in others.

Amen.

(IX) POWER AND CORRUPTION

Read: 2 Chronicles 9

367.

Lord, thank you for the warnings your word contains;
For the stories of failure that can help to guide us.
Teach us through the stories of David and Solomon
What power can do in the right and the wrong hands.

368.

If I should have power, Lord, make me responsible;
If I should have wealth, Lord, make me generous;
If I should be a leader, Lord, let me lead by example;
If I should be wise, Lord, may I keep looking to you.

(X) FAITH IN SUFFERING

Read: Job 1

369.

I am amazed and encouraged by the example of Job,
Whose faith persisted even when his world was being
    ripped apart.
Lord, throughout his suffering you silently sustained
    him;
Help us to remember that when pain and tragedy hit.

370.

Lord, through every high and low, sustain our faith;
Help us to keep going, even when we're in a place of
   darkness, fear or confusion.
When we are suffering, help us to see your light,
And, like Job, bring us safely out the other side.
Lord, make us persevering;
Give us endurance and persistence and never-say-die.
And as we stick with you, please, God, stick with us.

(XI) WORSHIP

Read: Psalm 23

371.

God, we worship you;
You made us and redeem us;
You are our beginning and our end.
You sent your Son to die for us and
You offer us eternity with you.
Nothing has ever existed, or will ever exist, that
   deserves even one per cent of the praise that is due
   to you;
The whole of nature cries out to you in an act of
   continuous worship.
So we, in our own humble way – tiny atoms in the
   context of your universe –
Choose to worship you today.
And the greatest miracle is that you hear our worship,
   and you love it.

372.

Lord, teach me what it is to live a life of worship, like
  David;
Make me a psalmist, my life a new book of psalms.
Show me what it is to worship you
Not only with my words,
But with my whole life.

(XII) WISDOM (AND GUIDANCE)

Read: Proverbs 3

373.

Thank you, Lord, for wisdom,
In others, in your word, and given directly from you.
Thank you that you do not leave us here alone, but
  that you guide us;
When the path is forked, we can come to you for help.
Be our map and our guide in everything.

374.

I ask, Lord, that I would be wiser,
That you would guide my heart, hands and feet.
Give me wisdom in every situation,
That I might make decisions that are right and which
  honour you.
As I listen to others, make me discerning;
As I come to speak, always enable me to think first.
Let me be known as someone who is wise,
Because I walk closely with you.

(XIII) A COMING MESSIAH

Read: Isaiah 9:1–7

375.

> I thank you, God, that sending your Son wasn't a
>   change of plan;
> It wasn't a knee-jerk reaction to a world spinning out
>   of control.
> God, you had always planned this;
> Your plans are perfect.
> The whole of history hangs and spins on his coming –
>   it wasn't an afterthought;
> Thank you that, as we assess your great story,
> We can see the great plotline of Jesus running straight
>   through the centre.

376.

> May I be filled with hope, Lord,
> Because you sent your Son to rescue me,
> Because Jesus is the centrepiece of everything.
> May the hope I have
> Be life-transforming,
> Be infectious,
> Be the driving force behind everything I do and say.

(XIV) RENEWAL

Read: Ezekiel 37

377.

> I praise you, God, because you do not give up on your
> people;
> Though Israel stumbled time and time again,
> Turned their backs on you even when you had been
> miraculously present among them,
> You did not turn away from them.
> Again and again, you rescue and renew;
> I worship the God who renews broken things.

378.

> God, you know where things aren't right in my life;
> You know where I am not living how I should be,
> where I am not honouring you.
> But these habits, they seem so hard to change, Lord;
> Without your power, I do not think I have the strength
> to overcome them.
> So I call on you, God of renewal, and humbly ask:
> Work in my heart, break the power of sin over me,
> And transform me over time into an unrecognizable
> version of myself,
> And a greater likeness of your Son.

(XV) PUNISHMENT AND RESTORATION

Read: Hosea 1

379.

Lord, we are sorry for when we are like the Israelites,
When we turn from you and worship idols.
We are sorry that money, sex, power, and selfishness
become more important to us
Even than our relationship with the Living God.
So, Lord, we are open to your correction;
Show us where we are going wrong,
And restore us as you restored your people Israel.

380.

God, when you ask us to take on more than it seems
possible to bear,
Give us the strength of character and presence of mind
To serve you regardless of the cost.

(XVI) GOD SENDS HIS SON

Read: Luke 2

381.

Into a fallen world, Jesus Christ, the Son of God,
was born;
Has there ever been a greater miracle?
Lord, our words run dry as we search for a response;
Accept our awe and wonder as worship and praise.

382.

Jesus, I want to know you personally,
Intimately, as a soulmate.
You came to this world, fully human,
Because you didn't want me to be left behind.
Now my desire is not to know you from afar, as a
  character in a story,
Or simply as a God to bow to,
But, even more than that, as a friend.

(XVII) JESUS' LINE

Read: Luke 3:21–37

383.

The line of man runs unbroken, from the fall of
Adam to the redeeming work of Jesus. As a story
that's incredible; as a reality it's miraculous. Lord, we
worship you.

384.

Help me to see, Lord, where I fit into your story;
Where my small life somehow weaves into the same
  plot that also features Jesus.
Show me the plans you have for my life;
Give me your mind as I navigate a path through it.
I ask that I would understand why the things I do
  matter, in this great scheme;
Why you should care about me, or the way I live my
  life.

In seeing more clearly, I pray that I would not be
content with an ordinary life,
But, in finding my place in your story,
Be part of a movement that changes the world.

(XVIII) DISCIPLESHIP

Read: Luke 5

385.

I thank you, God, that you call us to follow you;
That, as Jesus asked men to join in with what he was
doing then,
Still you make that same request to us now.
Lord, we are overwhelmed that you would want us as
your disciples,
Even after you know everything about us.
You called those fishermen to catch men instead,
And you extend that call to us;
We take it up with fear and trembling.

386.

I want to spend my life with you, Lord,
In step with your Spirit, journeying with you.
As you called your disciples, you have called to me;
I grab that invitation with both hands.
As I walk with you, please change me, inside and out,
Until I begin to reflect you to the world around me.

(XIX) PRAYER (AND FORGIVENESS)

Read: Matthew 6

387.

As our Saviour taught us, so we pray:

Our Father in heaven,
Hallowed be your name,
Your kingdom come,
Your will be done
On earth as it is in heaven.
Give us today our daily bread.
Forgive us our debts,
As we have also forgiven our debtors.
And lead us not into temptation,
But deliver us from the evil one.

388.

Lord, we are incredulous that you would listen to us;
Amazed that there is anything we could say that you
would want to hear.
Yet that is miraculously, impossibly, true.
Make us, then, people of prayer,
Who never neglect to speak to the God who lives in us
and watches us constantly.
In every situation, in every moment of our lives,
May we turn towards you in prayer and thanksgiving.

Amen.

[XX] HEALING

Read: Mark 8:22-26

389.

> We praise you, God of miracles,
> That when your Son walked the earth
> He walked in incomparable power,
> And brought you glory as he healed the sick.
> We thank you also that you are not finished;
> That you still heal today.
> Give us a faith that joins the dots between what was,
>   then,
> And what can still be, now.

390.

> God, you can heal our bodies,
> But you also heal the soul.
> Thank you for showing us the difference,
> And, while we often hope for the former,
> We ask first that you would grant us the latter.

[XXI] JESUS' DEATH AND RESURRECTION

Read: John 19:16 - 20:9

391.

> As we think about the defining weekend in human
>   history, Lord,
> As we consider the scale and impact of it all,
> We all but fall silent.

You allowed your only Son to die,
So that we could have life in eternity.
Without his sacrifice, we were hopeless;
In the darkness of that moment, hope broke through.
You redefined the laws of the universe in a moment;
In three days death itself was beaten.
With humble words, Lord, we worship you.
For what you have done, Jesus, we bow before you.
You are our King, and yet you put on flesh and gave
    yourself for us.
How incredible, how extraordinary, how great you
    are.

392.

Jesus, may we live in the light of your death and
    resurrection,
Dying to ourselves each day, and rising again in you.

(XXII) THE HOLY SPIRIT

Read: Acts 2

393.

For sending your Spirit at Pentecost, we thank you;
For the gifts of prophecy and tongues, and for
    countless other wonders, we praise you.
We worship you, our supernatural God,
Who does move in silence but in power,
Who transforms heart and mind through the work of
    your Spirit.

394.

Holy Spirit, point us towards Jesus;
Fill us with worship for our God and creator.
We welcome you into our hearts, as we consider the
    miracle that the power of God can rest within us,
We ask you to come into our hearts again and again;
Each day we dare to ask that you would be poured
    into us once more.
We want to be supernaturally charged people,
Powered by the God who is nearer than our breath.
Through your work within us, give us the spiritual
    tools to transform our world,
And lead us into an ever-deeper friendship with Jesus,
    our Saviour.

(XXIII) CHURCH

Read: Acts 4:32–37

395.

We thank you, God, for the church, the body of your
people here on earth, and the bride of Christ.

We thank you for the picture of the early church, and
ask that you would send us backwards, so that we
now might better resemble our forefathers in the way
we love one another.

396.

Lord, help me to relate to church;
Sometimes it feels so alien to my culture.

I pray that I would discover for myself the simplicity
and ideals of the church as it was first established,
And, with your wisdom, be part of a generation that
reimagines church in unity and in love.
God, help me to remain on the inside even when it
would be easier to walk away,
And fill me with grace as I struggle with the way
things are.

(XXIV) PAUL

Read: Philippians 1

397.

God, we give you thanks for the life and teaching of
your servant Paul,
Who stopped at nothing to see your message
preached;
Who suffered in chains for your sake and died for
your cause;
Who sought to lead by example,
And who placed faith in others to drive the gospel on.
We thank you for his life and the chance to read
about it.
Even more we praise you because his efforts were not
in vain;
Because the good news he preached wasn't an idea,
but truth:
Jesus Christ really did die, really was raised, really
does live.

398.

Make me like Paul,
With a passion to see my friends know you,
A determination that doesn't know when it's beaten,
And a desire to become more holy.

Amen.

(XXV) LIFE AFTER DEATH

Read: Revelation 21

399.

Thank you, God, for letting us in on the end of the
   story,
For giving us a vision of the way things will be.
God, we cannot begin to thank you for the chance to
   live eternally;
Our heads cannot comprehend the idea that we will
   not die.
Yet that is what you offer:
Through your resurrected Son you offer us life that
   does not end;
Eternity in your presence.
We worship you because you are victorious over evil,
   and even over death.
We praise you because you are God eternal, our King.

400.

Help me, Lord, to comprehend eternity with you,
That I might lead others there also.

Seasons and occasions

There are certain moments when prayer is utterly appropriate but often forgotten. These aren't necessarily times when we're struggling, suffering or in need of something, but simply when the calendar presents us with an opportunity to remember God in thanks. I don't know about you, but, despite the fact that they are "churchy" times of the year, I often get so caught up in the rituals of Christmas and Easter – religious and otherwise – that I forget to spend time with God. Then on my own birthday, a time when I should surely be giving thanks for all the amazing ways that God has blessed me, I usually busy myself so much with having fun that I don't even check in with him to say "hi". Can you imagine how sad your parents would be if you didn't even bother to check in with them on your birthday? These prayers take those three occasions, Christmas, Easter and our own birthday, and provide a few words to make sure that religion and celebration don't end up pushing God to the margins.

CHRISTMAS

401. A Christmas Eve prayer

Loving Father, help us remember the birth of Jesus,
that we may share in the song of the angels,
the gladness of the shepherds,
and worship of the wise men.
Close the door of hate and open the door of love all
  over the world.
Let kindness come with every gift and good desires
  with every greeting.
Deliver us from evil by the blessing which Christ
  brings, and teach us to be merry with clear hearts.
May the Christmas morning make us happy to be thy
  children, and Christmas evening bring us to our beds
  with grateful thoughts, forgiving and forgiven, for
  Jesus' sake. Amen.

Robert Louis Stevenson (1850–94)

402. Expectant night

On Christmas Eve, Lord, make me expectant,
Not for gifts of more unnecessary stuff,
But for the gift of your Son,
Who came to earth and turned it upside down.

403. A Christmas creed

I believe in Jesus, and I believe in the incredible gospel
Which begins in Bethlehem.
I believe in the God whose Spirit glorified a little town;
Whose Spirit continues to bring music to people all
  over the world, in cities, towns and villages.

I believe in the one for whom there was no room at
   the inn,
And I confess that sometimes,
My heart still cannot find room for Him today.
I believe in Him – ignored by 'wise men' and rulers;
Whom the proud could never quite understand;
Whose life was lived at the heart of common community,
Who was welcomed by those with hungry hearts.
I believe in Him – the one who proclaimed
the love of God to be invincible.
I believe in the one whose cradle was a mother's arms,
Who lived in a modest home in Nazareth,
Full of love but little wealth;
Who looked at humble people and made them see
What God's love saw in them;
Who through His love rescued sinners,
And lifted up human weakness
To meet the strength of God.
I confess that I need God – now and forever:
For forgiveness of my selfishness and greed,
For new life for my empty soul,
For love in a heart grown cold.
I believe in God, who gives us the very best of himself.
I believe in Jesus, who is the Son of the living God,
Who is born in Bethlehem this night,
Not just for me but for the whole world.

Based on a prayer by Walter Russell Bowie (1882–1969)

404. Prayer to the vulnerable God

Lord Jesus, we worship you at Christmas
Because you, majestic and everlasting,
Came to live among us and made yourself vulnerable.

From the safety of heaven,
You came to earth,
And took on the humble flesh of a man.
Not only that, but, though you didn't deserve to die,
You accepted the walk to the cross and died at the
    hands of men,
Shattered the power of death as you rose again,
And now sit again at the right hand of your Father,
Still involved on earth, still engaged,
Still making yourself vulnerable each day,
As you offer yourself to us.
What a Saviour you are. We bow before you.

405. Nativity prayer

Let the just rejoice,
for their Justifier is born.
Let the sick and infirm rejoice,
For their Saviour is born.
Let the captives rejoice,
For their Redeemer is born.
Let slaves rejoice,
for their Master is born.
Let free men rejoice,
For their Liberator is born.
Let all Christians rejoice,
For Jesus Christ is born.

St Augustine of Hippo (354–430)

406. What would I see?

If I could look into that manger, what would I see?
Would I recognize the Son of God,
Or would I see only a child, given the birth of a

pauper?
Help me, Lord Jesus, to see you for who you really are,
And never to miss the work of the divine in the midst
of the ordinary.

407. As a small child

Let Your goodness, Lord, appear to us, that we,
made in Your image, conform ourselves to it.
In our own strength
we cannot imitate Your majesty, power, and wonder,
nor is it fitting for us to try.
But Your mercy reaches from the heavens
through the clouds to the earth below.
You have come to us as a small child,
but You have brought us the greatest of all gifts,
the gift of eternal love.
Caress us with Your tiny hands,
embrace us with Your tiny arms
and pierce our hearts with Your soft, sweet cries.

St Bernard of Clairvaux (1090–1153)

408. Exchange of gifts

You gave to us your only Son, born to die for me;
My gift to you is all I have – my heart and soul for
thee.

409. Prayer for Christmas Day

The feast day of Your birth resembles You, Lord,
Because it brings joy to all humanity.
Old people and infants alike enjoy Your day.

Your day is celebrated
from generation to generation.
Kings and emperors may pass away,
And the festivals to commemorate them soon lapse.
But Your festival
will be remembered until the end of time.
Your day is a means and a pledge of peace.
At Your birth heaven and earth were reconciled,
Since You came from heaven to earth on that day
You forgave our sins and wiped away our guilt.
You gave us so many gifts on the day of Your birth:
A treasure chest of spiritual medicines for the sick;
Spiritual light for the blind;
The cup of salvation for the thirsty;
The bread of life for the hungry.
In the winter when trees are bare,
You give us the most succulent spiritual fruit.
In the frost when the earth is barren,
You bring new hope to our souls.
In December when seeds are hidden in the soil,
The staff of life springs forth from the virgin womb.

St Ephraim the Syrian (306–73)

410. Real Christmas

May the world know a difference in me this
   Christmas, Lord;
Would you so enlighten and shine through me that I'm
not just the same as I was before I met you;
As my mouth talks of a "real" meaning to Christmas,
May my hands and feet demonstrate the truth of it.
May people see in me not just another consumer,
But one consumed with the love of God.

411. Sweet Child of Bethlehem

O sweet Child of Bethlehem,
grant that we may share with all our hearts
in this profound mystery of Christmas.
Put into the hearts of men and women this peace
for which they sometimes seek so desperately
and which you alone can give to them.
Help them to know one another better,
and to live as brothers and sisters,
children of the same Father.
Reveal to them also your beauty, holiness and purity.
Awaken in their hearts
love and gratitude for your infinite goodness.
Join them all together in your love.
And give us your heavenly peace. Amen.

Pope John XXIII (1881–1963)

412. Incarnation

*Incarnation simply means that God became fully human in the person
of Jesus – literally that God "took on flesh". We too can "incarnate"
Jesus by living like him in our homes, schools and communities, and in
this way Jesus takes on our flesh too. This prayer addresses both ideas.*

Lord Jesus Christ, who came to earth as a baby,
Help us to understand exactly what that meant;
Open our eyes to just how fully human you became,
How much you exposed yourself for us.
May we know the power of your incarnation,
And so incarnate you here today,
Living like you among those we love,
So that they might see you in us, and so realize
That you are alive, and worth living for.

413. For those who have little

At Christmas, never let my thoughts be far from those
who have little.
As I feast on a lunch that could make me sick, remind
me of those who are sick with hunger;
As I tear off the wrapping on another gift, let me be
moved to identify with those who have nothing to
open.
Lord, I will not stop at saying that you are God of the
rich and the poor;
God, move me beyond feeling bad and stir me into
acts of response.
May the excesses of Christmas be a catalyst for change
in my heart.

414. Peace prayer

God of peace, bring an end to conflict;
Cease war;
Still arguments.
In far-off places, in my nation, in my home, in my
heart,
Lord, bring peace.

415. Christmas blessing

God grant us the light of Christmas,
which is faith;
the warmth of Christmas,
which is purity;
the righteousness of Christmas,
which is justice;
the belief in Christmas,

which is truth;
the all of Christmas,
which is Christ.

Wilda English

EASTER

416. Living resurrection

Jesus, you died, but you rose again;
Now you live in me, through the Spirit.
May my life reflect not death, but resurrection;
Give me joy, not sorrow;
And make me good news to the people around me
As I live, filled up with the power of rebirth.

417. As I picture...

As I picture
The blunt and filthy nails driven into your hands and
    feet,
The crown of thorns forced agonizingly down on your
    head,
The shaming words of insult and abuse lashed upon
    you,
The terrible final breaths, each one harder than the
    last,
My heart weeps.

Thank you,
Lord Jesus,
that you went through that
For me.

418. Christ is Risen

Christ is Risen: The world below lies desolate
Christ is Risen: The spirits of evil are fallen
Christ is Risen: The angels of God are rejoicing
Christ is Risen: The tombs of the dead are empty
Christ is Risen indeed from the dead,
The first of the sleepers,
Glory and power are his for ever and ever.

St Hippolytus

419. All is not lost

Jesus, as you died, hope seemed to die with you;
The Messiah, killed by man.
And yet in three days you turned the story on its head,
Proved yourself the Messiah that no one expected;
Returned not as a vision but as flesh and blood.
So when hope seems lost,
I will live in the light of you,
Knowing that, however bad it seems, all is not lost;
And that, in the end, love wins.

420. Magnificent and radiant

This wonderful prayer of Saint Gregory takes us to the heart of Easter, and to the point of why Jesus died on the cross. This is what it's all about!

It is only right,
with all the powers of our heart and mind,
to praise You, Father,
and Your Only-begotten Son,
Our Lord Jesus Christ:

Dear Father, by Your wondrous condescension of
  loving-kindness towards us, Your servants,
You gave up your Son.
Dear Jesus, You paid the debt of Adam for us to the
  Eternal Father
By Your Blood poured forth in loving-kindness.
You cleared away the darkness of sin
By Your magnificent and radiant Resurrection.
You broke the bonds of death
and rose from the grave as a Conqueror.
You reconciled heaven and earth.
Our life had no hope of eternal happiness
before You redeemed us.
Your Resurrection has washed away our sins,
restored our innocence and brought us joy.
How inestimable is the tenderness
of Your love!

St Gregory the Great (540–604)

421. You faced death

Though we know darkness, you knew it more severely
  than any of us;
Though we face fears and difficulties, you faced death.
As I try to walk through the challenging times,
I will do it by following you.

422. It is finished

On the cross you cried:
"It is finished!"
And then you gave up your last breath.
Lord, those words,

And the agony you felt in speaking them,
Are beyond our comprehension.
All we can do is say thank you.

423. Prayer of new life

In the light of your resurrection, Lord Jesus,
I accept the new life you offer me, grasp it with all
    my might,
And so enter into communion with God himself,
Who forgives me, accepts me, draws near to me and
    loves me,
With a love so brilliant it could blind;
A love so great that it surrounds and engulfs.
This is what Easter means;
This is what the stakes were:
Because of Jesus' death and resurrection,
I can know God as a friend.

424. Easter-egg prayer

Like melting chocolate,
Melt away the façade of what Easter has become,
And lead us to the truth of your Son,
Who died and rose again.

Like a foil wrapper that tears away,
Tear off the wrapping around our hearts,
So that we might know the miracle of Easter,
And so realize the greatest gift of all.

425. Raise up and renew

God our Father,
by raising Christ your Son
you conquered the power of death
and opened for us the way to eternal life.
Let our celebration today
raise us up and renew our lives
by the Spirit that is within us.

Traditional Catholic prayer

BIRTHDAYS

426. Birthday prayer

For another year, Lord, I am grateful;
For the year ahead I am expectant.
Take this year; take my life,
And do something spectacular with it.

427. Sixteenth-birthday prayer

Thank you, Lord, for bringing me this far;
As my life changes gear, I pray you'd remain at the
  heart of it.
As temptations increase, give me self-control;
As pressures grow, give me peace and resilience;
As opportunities enlarge, give me wisdom,
And, as I journey towards adulthood,
Keep alive in me the faith of a little child.

428. Eighteenth-birthday prayer

As I stand on the threshold of adult life,
I thank you for everything that's gone before,
And look ahead with excitement to all that lies ahead.
Lord God, I pray that, as the world now honours me
    with responsibility,
You would help me to act in a way that honours you.
May I walk a path of responsibility with the things I
    consume,
A way of respect and integrity in relationships,
A route of integrity and involvement with politics.
Bring me, Lord, to full maturity in you,
And start today.

429. For a friend's birthday

Lord, I pray a blessing over my friend today,
That she would know how much she is loved,
And know you close by.

Amen.

430. On a sad anniversary

Lord, on this day I ask that you would draw near to
    me and comfort me,
And do the same for everyone who is feeling like me.
When once this day brought happiness, now its
    remembrance brings tears.
Lord, understand me as no one else can;
Take my grief as a kind of worship,
A testament to the love you have placed within me,
And give me some small sense of resolution,
And a greater faith that you are in control.

Community prayers

This last section is designed for use in group and community settings. That could mean a church service, or it might mean a small group of friends who want to say a few prayers at the end of an evening together. Because I want it to be really useful, I've squeezed in four styles of prayer in one section!

The first twenty-five are intended for use in conjunction with well-known songs and hymns, although they can of course be used completely on their own. How this might work, then, is that after (or before) singing the relevant song together, one of you reads the prayer as a kind of response, or to earth the meaning of some of the words in the song. I know that for me it can sometimes be very easy to sing songs without really considering their intended meaning; these prayers might help to overcome that problem.

After that, I've included fifteen very short prayers, which could be used as an aid to meditation, or even as a chant.

If that seems at all weird, be reassured that Christians have been chanting simple, biblically based and affirming lines like these for hundreds of years.

Third, there are some liturgies, which are simply prayers to be read together. Again, this is an ancient and completely sound practice, which allows Christians to agree together their thoughts about God, their hopes, and their faith.

Finally, I wanted to close the book in a fitting way, with ten prayers of blessing. Often we fall into a fairly religious pattern in respect of the way we end things and say goodbye – many churches end their services with the same words each week. These blessings attempt to add a little bit of variety to the way we affirm and dismiss one another.

In the twenty-first century we often think of Christianity as an individualistic faith – all about "me and God". In fact, God himself has always dealt with communities – from his people Israel to his church today – and even lives in community himself, in the Holy Trinity. These prayers are here to balance out the individual focus of the rest of this book, by providing just a few words that we can enjoy praying together.

PRAYERS FOR COMMUNITY WORSHIP

431. For the Spirit of worship

Almighty God, from whom every good prayer comes,
And who pours out on all who desire it the Spirit of
   grace and worship,
Deliver us, when we draw near to you,
From coldness of heart and wanderings of mind;
That with focused thoughts and stirring passion,
We may worship you in spirit and in truth;
Through Jesus Christ our Lord. Amen.

Based on a prayer by William Bright (1824 –1901)

432. Connects with: "Amazing grace" [J. Newton]

Lord God, your grace is indescribable;
It is everything that we don't deserve.
As we – your people – are struck by the awesome
  realization
That your love is what gives sight to the blind
And leads your lost children home,
We pray that your grace, poured so lavishly on us,
Would overflow from us and into our community,
That others would see what "amazing" truly means,
And that they too might join with us in eternity,
  singing your praise,
Our voices never expiring.

433. Connects with: "Oh happy day" [T. Hughes]

We praise you, Jesus, for all you have done for us!
No words can describe how amazing it is to be set free
  from our sins;
We thank you for choosing to die for each and every
  one of us.

When we feel far away from you,
When we feel ashamed of things we have done,
Help us to remember the truth of this song;
Everything we have done wrong can be washed away
  because of what you did.

Sean Skinner

434. Connects with: "Blessed be your name"
[M. Redman]

In the best of times and in the worst of times,
Lord, we still make that choice to bless your name,
To worship you,
Because, whatever is going on in our lives, you are still
    worthy of our worship.
We will praise you when things go well,
We will remember your goodness to us.
Then, when suffering comes, we will not forget who
    you are.
Even when it hurts to say anything at all,
In our darkest hour, we will still find strength to say:
"My Saviour lives."

435. Connects with: "How deep the Father's love for us" [S. Townend]

Father,
How deep your love is for us;
Help us to understand even in part
The cost of that day,
As you gave up your only Son
To bring us life and forgiveness.
And as you turned your face away
We can't even imagine the pain
It must have caused you
To see your Son tortured and sacrificed.

And, Lord, as you hung on that cross
To pay the price for our sins
And as you endured the mocking and cursing from
the crowd below,

You could hear our voices echoed in their cries
And it drives us to our knees in shame.

We thank you, Lord,
That it is finished,
That in your dying breath you brought me life;
The price was paid
And by your wounds I was healed.

436. Connects with: "How great is our God"
(C. Tomlin, J. Reeves, E. Cash)

Lord, your greatness is overwhelming;
Though we know your glory in part now,
One day we know we'll see the full mind-blowing
    extent of it.
Where you are present, there is no place for darkness;
Your brilliance extinguishes evil;
And so we can only worship you, God,
With our mouths, but even more with our hearts,
Which continue to praise you even when our words
    run dry.

437. Connects with: "Consuming fire" (T. Hughes)

Father, we long for a deeper connection with you;
We're tired of playing at this.
We want to be Spirit-filled and God-inspired;
We want to see our communities changed
Because we have been changed.
So, Lord, have your way with us;
Consume us; purify us,
For your glory's sake.

Amen.

438. Connects with: "Your grace is enough"
[M. Maher, C. Tomlin]

Thank you, God, for your amazing love.

Thank you for sticking by us, even when our hearts
   are far from you.

Remind us that your grace and love are all that we
   need;
That your love can see us through any situation, even
   when we are at our weakest.

Sean Skinner

439. Connects with: "Be thou my vision"
[M. Byrne, E. Hull]

High King of heaven,
Ruler of all,
Lord of my heart,
You are everything to me.
I ask that you would invade and take over every part
   of me,
So that I would better resemble my King.
God, be in my eyes, my hands and feet, my
   understanding,
And draw me daily closer to yourself,
So that I might see you, feel you and know you more
   clearly,
Today more than yesterday, and every day into
   eternity.

Amen.

440. Connects with: "You bled" (Rend Collective Experiment)

> You chose to leave your perfection,
> You chose to embrace our rejection.
> How extraordinary a sacrifice,
> How astonishing a Saviour.
>
> You fought for our redemption.
> How remarkable a love,
> How incredible a friend.

441. Connects with: "This is our God" (R. Morgan)

You may wish to encourage worshippers to sit or kneel after this song, and leave a good-length break between each phrase.

> God, we fall at your feet;
> We are struck silent by your presence.
>
> God, we fall at your feet;
> We find our rest in you.
>
> God, we fall at your feet;
> There is nothing we can say or do to make you love us
>   more.
>
> God, we fall at your feet;
> You redeem us and restore us; you are our Saviour.
>
> God, we fall at your feet;
> As your Son surrendered his life on that cross, so we
>   surrender to you now.

442. Connects with: "Tell out, my soul!"

(T. Dudley-Smith)

My soul praises God,
My spirit rejoices in him,
That he would choose to think of me,
That he would care about me.
He has done great things
In my life, and in the lives of his people;
His mercy is like a mighty wave;
The effects of his grace are felt for generations.
He scatters the proud; he can bring down
    governments in a second,
Yet he lifts up the humble; he sustains the broken-
    hearted.
Just as he promised Abraham, he will never give up
    on his people.
My soul sings, because this is my God.

Based on Luke 1:46–55 (Mary's "Magnificat")

443. Connects with: "You're beautiful"

(P. Wickham)

Lord Jesus, your beauty is not an abstract thing but a
    reality;
The person you are is beautiful,
The things that you have done for us are beautiful.
Whether hanging, beaten, on a cross
Or resurrected in glory,
Your beauty has never been in question.
So we long for the day when we can see you face
    to face,

When we can stand before you and tell you with our
　own words
How beautiful you are.
But until that day we will go on worshipping you
　here on earth,
Paying tribute to our beautiful Saviour.

444. Connects with: "Everything" [T. Hughes]

Christ in me, the hope of glory,
Lord, be in every part of me.
And may I so radiate your light
That every eye that sees me sees Christ also.

Amen.

445. Connects with: "Everlasting God"
[B. Brown, K. Riley]

I ask, God, that I would feel your presence
　surrounding me,
That I would know your amazing love when I need
　comforting,
That you would look after me and guide me through
　the tricky situations that I face.
Lord, as I lift you up in worship, I humbly ask that
　you would lift me up.
I know that you will never falter; you will never fail.

Sean Skinner

446. Connects with: "Here is love" [W. Rees]

Our world was guilty,
And yet you kissed it with love.
We want to respond to that love with what little we
  have,
With our mouths, our hearts and our lives.
Lord, foster in us the same love for others
That you first had for us;
Because you first loved us,
We want to return that love and share it.

447. Connects with: "O praise him" [D. Crowder]

We join in with the angels as they sing:
Holy, Holy, Holy God,
Heaven and earth are full of your glory.
We are simple, broken, sinful and insignificant,
Yet you love our praise.
We praise you, God;
We praise you, Jesus, our Saviour.

448. Connects with: "Before the throne of God above" [C. Bancroft]

As we stand before your throne today
We are lost for words,
Overwhelmed by your love for us.

And as we lift our pleas and prayers up to you
We stand as those who are forgiven and loved,
Who belong to the King of glory and grace,
Our Saviour – the Lord, Jesus Christ –
Who rescued us from our sin.

And as we battle against Satan's lies
And the way he tries to discourage us
and tell us we're just not good enough,
Help us to remember that our lives are hidden in you;
That the battle is already won.
My soul has already been purchased
And I now belong to you,
Unchanging God.

Laura Haddow

449. Connects with: "On Christ the solid rock"
(E. Mote)

Jesus, you are the rock on which my faith is built,
The ground on which my life is pitched.
There is no other place I would want to be,
No other hope that could sustain me;
Your presence is all.
In the uncertainty of this world, it is you I return to
again and again.
I keep coming back to you, because you are my home.
On you, Lord, I will stand;
All other ground is sinking sand.

450. Connects with: "Here I am to worship"
(T. Hughes)

I'll never know or understand the agony of the cross;
I'll never know or understand how it felt for the
Father;
I'll never know or understand how much it took for
you to stay there, Jesus,
To see it through for our sake.

But I will worship you – for the rest of my life,
I will worship you with everything I am.
Here I am, Lord; I give myself completely to you.

451. Connects with: "In Christ alone" (S. Townend)

The power of Christ lives in me.
This is what I wholeheartedly believe.
Help me not to hide or shade the light of the world,
But through me may it lead others to you
Until you return or call me home.

Amen.

452. Connects with: "How He loves"
[J. M. McMillan]

God, your love is indescribable, inexplicable;
It extends further, and wider, and longer, and deeper
 than we can comprehend;
It knows no boundaries, it advances relentlessly;
It cannot be calculated, it cannot be quantified;
It exceeds any measure and explodes any metaphor.
It is in every sense glorious, in every way magnificent.
And this is the love that you pour out on us;
This is the love that you lavish upon us.

453. Connects with: "When I survey" [I. Watts]

"Love so amazing, so divine,
Demands my soul, my life, my all."
God, we want to live by those words,
We want to respond to your amazing love
By giving you everything we are.

As we consider the cross,
There is nothing less we could offer.
Did ever such love and sorrow meet as on that day?
Lord Jesus, we can only worship you.

454. Connects with: "Our God is mercy" (B. Brown)

Lord God, you are our refuge.
When we're lonely,
When we're broken,
When we're only just holding it together,
God, you are hope.

455. Connects with: "Faithful one" (B. Doerksen)

Thank you, Lord, that you hear us
Even in the midst of a storm.
In times of trouble, fear and doubt
Your love is the anchor that will hold us;
Your faithfulness is the rock we can stand upon.
Thank you that you lift us up when we fall.
Unchanging God,
We thank you for the hope and peace you place deep
within our hearts.

Laura Haddow

CHANTS AND MICRO-PRAYERS

456. The Jesus Prayer

Lord Jesus Christ,
Son of God,
have mercy on me,
a sinner.

Traditional

457. While we were sinners

God demonstrates his own love for us in this:
While we were still sinners, Christ died for us.

Romans 5:8

458. Holy God

Perfect, flawless, Holy God,
You draw near to us,
And we worship you.

459. Give us your heart

Give us your heart for the people around us,
That we may love them as you do.

460. Stay

Stay with us, O Lord Jesus Christ, night will soon fall.
Then stay with us, O Lord Jesus Christ, light in our
   darkness.

The Taizé community

461. Greater

Though our problems seem great, you are greater;
We release them to you.

462. Live for ever

We will not die; in Christ we live for ever.

463. Peace

Grant us your peace, O Lord; may it fill all our days.

The Taizé community

464. Lost sons

When we were still a long way off, you saw us, and
ran towards us with your arms wide open.

465. Timber of the cross

Behold the timber of the cross on which
Salvation of the world was suspended.

Come to adore him!

Gregorian chant

466. Hear me

Hear my prayer, let my cry come to you.
You, God, remain for ever.

The Taizé community

467. East to west

As far as the east is from the west,
so far has he removed our transgressions from us.

Psalm 103:12

468. Holy Spirit

Fill us, Holy Spirit; renew us, Holy Spirit; transform
us, Holy Spirit.

469. Your light shines

Lord Jesus Christ, your light shines within us;
Let not my doubts or my darkness speak to me.
Lord Jesus Christ, your light shines within us;
Let my heart always welcome your love.

The Taizé community

470. God of justice

God of justice, open our eyes to the need around us.
And put us to your work.

PRAYERS AND LITURGIES TO SAY TOGETHER

471. A prayer for the church

Most gracious Father,
we pray to you for your holy catholic church.
Fill it with all truth,
in all truth with all peace.

Where it is corrupt, purge it.
Where it is in error, direct it.
Where it is superstitious, rectify it.
Where anything is amiss, reform it.
Where it is right, strengthen and defend it.
Where it is in want, provide for it.
Where it is divided, heal it and reunite it in your love;
for the sake of your Son, our Saviour Jesus Christ.

William Laud (1573–1645)

472. Take us, use us

Lord God,
Creator of heaven and earth,
We stand before you as people
Broken by the world but reassembled by your hands;
Take us as we are;
Use us in your plan
To remake, renew and reimagine
This shattered world.

Amen.

473. No hands but yours

Christ has no body now but yours.
No hands, no feet on earth but yours.
Yours are the eyes through which he looks
With compassion on this world.
Let nothing disturb you.
Let nothing frighten you.
All things pass away:
God never changes.

Patience obtains all things.
Those who have God
Find they lack nothing;
God alone suffices.

St Teresa of Avila (1515–82)

474. Lord of all

Lord of majesty, reign over us;
Lord of intimacy, reign within us;
Lord of service, open our hands;
Lord of love, open our hearts.

475. Prayer of youth

O God, our Heavenly Father,
In life's morning we come to you for guidance through
  its entire day.
Help us always to follow Jesus in the paths of
  righteousness.
Keep us in your love, that we may glorify you in our
  labour and our life.
Bless us with health and strength and purity,
And give us a will to serve you in every good work,
So that we may make a better world for all people to
  live in here,
And become worthy of your presence in a brighter
  world hereafter.

Bishop Murray

476. Use us together

Use us together, Lord;
Draw us close as your people,
Put us to work in your world as one,
Add more to our number,
And bring glory to yourself.

477. A measure of your Spirit

O Lord Jesus Christ,
give us a measure of your Spirit
that we may be enabled to obey your teaching:
to pacify anger,
to take part in pity,
to moderate desire,
to increase love,
to put away sorrow,
to cast away vainglory,
not to be vindictive,
not to fear death;
ever entrusting our spirit to the immortal God
who with you and the Holy Spirit lives and reigns,
world without end.

St Apollonius (170–245)

478. All-day God

God, in our morning, bless us as we rise;
God, in our afternoon, put us to work for you;
God, in our evening, give us good rest;
God, in our night-time, watch over us,
Until tomorrow.

479. God in me

God be in my head
and in my understanding.
God be in my eyes
and in my looking.
God be in my mouth
and in my speaking.
God be in my heart
and in my thinking.
God be at my end
and at my departing.

From the Sarum Book of Hours (1514)

480. For generosity

Lord, your word says we are to be living sacrifices,
To give you access to every area of our lives and
  hearts.
As part of our worship to you
We lift to you all our passions, gifts, and skills,
And we pray that in some way,
Even though they may be small,
You can take them and use them for your glory,
To help build your church and serve others.

Please help us also in the ways we use our time and
  our money.
You bless us abundantly with these things;
Help us to give them back to you
Willingly and generously.
We pray that you will have your way in our lives.

481. For us, for them

Into your hands, merciful Lord, we commend ourselves for this day; may we be aware of your presence until its end; remind us that in whatever good we do we are serving you; make us careful and watchful, so that in everything we may discern your will, and, knowing it, may gladly obey.

Almighty and everlasting God, the comfort of the sad, the strength of those who suffer; hear the prayers of your children who cry out of any trouble; and to every distressed soul grant mercy, relief and refreshment.

From the Gelasian Sacramentary (eighth century)

482. Praying as one for the persecuted

There is something profound about praying with other believers for the suffering, persecuted church. This prayer might work especially well in a congregational setting, as the local church joins together to pray for the wider church.

Heavenly Father,
We thank you for the freedom we have in meeting
  together here.
Thank you that as we pray,
Lift our praises to you in worship,
And meet around your word,
We can do so without the fear of being harmed,
  imprisoned, and even put to death.
Lord, help us not to take this freedom for granted
But to thank you every day for it.

Lord, we pray for those across this world who love
  you but who are living in places where your church
  is persecuted,

Who risk everything to belong to you.
You know each one of them by name.
Please be close to them today;
Fill them with the assurance that you are there with
    them,
And that we are praying for them.
Thank you for their bravery and willingness to declare
    their love for you openly,
Even though it could cost them so much.
We lift them to you, and pray for protection, courage
    and an overwhelming sense of your presence to be
    with them today.

Laura Haddow

483. Trinitarian prayer

O Father,
your power is greater than all powers.
O Son,
under your leadership we cannot fear anything.
O Spirit,
under your protection there is nothing we cannot
    overcome.

Prayer of the Kikuyu, Kenya

484. God our light, life and strength

You, God, are the light of the minds that know you,
the life of the souls that love you,
and the strength of the wills that serve you;
Help us to know you so that we may truly love you,
And to love you so that we may fully serve you,
whom to serve is perfect freedom.

Watch, dear Lord, with those who wake, or watch, or weep tonight, and let your angels protect those who sleep. Tend the sick. Refresh the weary. Sustain the dying. Calm the suffering. Pity the distressed. We ask this for the sake of your love.

Lord Jesus, our Saviour, let us come to you.
Our hearts are cold; Lord, warm them with your
selfless love.
Our hearts are sinful; cleanse them with your precious
blood.
Our hearts are weak; strengthen them with your
joyous Spirit.
Our hearts are empty; fill them with your divine
presence.
Lord Jesus, our hearts are yours; possess them always
and only for yourself.

Based on a prayer by St Augustine of Hippo (354–430)

485. Prayer of unity

Lord,
We thank you that as believers in you we are one;
One with you,
One with each other.

Thank you for the gift of life you have given to us,
For the work you have done in us to change and
rescue us from an eternity without you.
As brothers and sisters in one family,
Help us to share each other's joys and struggles;
To pray for one another,
And to love and support each other in a way that
pleases you.

Lord,
As we long to share you with those around us who
    don't yet know you,
Help us to live lives that mirror yours,
That reflect you, even in a small way;
Plant in us a desire to share our faith with others
And give us the courage to speak out for you.
Thank you that even in our weakness you can use us
    to do amazing things.

486. God 360°

God to enfold me,
God to surround me,
God in my speaking,
God in my thinking.
God in my sleeping,
God in my waking,
God in my watching,
God in my hoping.
God in my life,
God in my lips,
God in my soul,
God in my heart.
God in my sufficing,
God in my slumber,
God in my ever-living soul,
God in mine eternity.

Translated from the **Carmina Gadelica** by Alexander
Carmichael (1832–1912)

487. For trust

Lord, increase my faith,
So that as I move towards you as your child,
I may trust where I cannot see, and hope where all
 seems doubtful,
Always looking to you as Father – in full control of all
 things,
And patiently doing the work you have given me
 to do;
According to the word of your Son, Jesus Christ.

Based on a prayer by George Dawson (1821–76)

488. The cross is...

The cross is the hope of Christians
the cross is the resurrection of the dead
the cross is the way of the lost
the cross is the saviour of the lost
the cross is the staff of the lame
the cross is the guide of the blind
the cross is the strength of the weak
the cross is the doctor of the sick
the cross is the aim of the priests
the cross is the hope of the hopeless
the cross is the freedom of the slaves
the cross is the power of the kings
the cross is the water of the seeds
the cross is the consolation of the bondmen
the cross is the source of those who seek water
the cross is the cloth of the naked.
We thank you, Father, for the cross.

Tenth-century African hymn

489. In everything

In all our thoughts, may we think of you;
In all our words, may we speak of you;
In all our actions, may we act as you;
In all our interactions, may we love like you;
In everything, may we look like you,
More and more each day.

Amen.

490. A covenant with God

The Methodist Covenant Prayer

I am no longer my own but yours.
Put me to what you will,
rank me with whom you will;
put me to doing, put me to suffering;
let me be employed for you or laid aside for you,
exalted for you or brought low for you.
Let me be full, let me be empty,
let me have all things, let me have nothing.
I freely and wholeheartedly yield all things
to your pleasure and disposal.
And now, glorious and blessed God,
Father, Son and Holy Spirit,
you are mine and I am yours.
So be it.
And the covenant made on earth,
let it be ratified in heaven.

Amen.

John Wesley (1703–91)

BLESSINGS AND BENEDICTIONS

491. Courage, wisdom and power

Take from us, O God, all pride and vanity, all boasting
and self-assertion, and give us the true courage that
shows itself in gentleness, the true wisdom that shows
itself in simplicity, and the true power that shows
itself in modesty.

Charles Kingsley (1819–75)

492. Walk in miracles

God of miracles, we long to see you glorified here,
In our time, in this place, in miraculous ways;
Increase our faith, our hunger, our love for each other,
So that we might dare to ask you to work miracles in
    and through us.

493. To walk without stumbling

God of love, the true sun of the world, eternally risen
and never going down; in your mercy shine into our
hearts, that the night of sin and the mists of error
being banished, we may, this day and all our life, walk
without stumbling along the way which you have set
before us.

Desiderius Erasmus (1466–1536)

494. Might we reflect

Lord, might we reflect, however dimly,
The image of your Son,
In our homes, our families, our friendships and our
    communities,
That they might know you calling to them also.

495. A blessing for the short of breath

May he support us all the day long till the shades
lengthen and the evening comes, and the busy world
is hushed, and the fever of life is over, and our work is
done. Then in his mercy may he give us a safe lodging,
and a holy rest and peace at the last.

John Henry Newman (1801–90)

496. Lord, go with us

Lord, go with us, and be:
The whispering voice of wisdom in our ears;
The calming source of patience in our souls;
The overflowing fountain of love in our hearts;
And remain all these things until we meet again,
So that we may share in the joy of your hand at work
    in our lives.

497. A blessing on each other

May you know God tonight,
Closer in your chest than breathing,
More surely than your heartbeat,
More certainly than you know your own strength.

God be in your mind and every sinew of your body;
God be in your heart and in your every breath.
God fill you up, and come pouring out of you.

Amen.

498. King eternal

O God, the King eternal,
whose light divides the day from the night
and turns the shadow of death into the morning:
Drive far from us all wrong desires,
incline our hearts to keep your law,
and guide our feet into the way of peace;
that, having done your will with cheerfulness
during the day, we may, when night comes,
rejoice to give you thanks;
through Jesus Christ our Lord.

Roman Catholic benediction – the Collect for Purity

499. As you go

As you go from here,
May your God go with you,
Shine a light on your path,
And lead you into a deeper friendship with himself,
So that you might better know his heart,
And feel your own being renewed.

500. Gaelic blessing

May the road rise up to meet you.
May the wind be always at your back.
May the sun shine warm upon your face;
the rains fall soft upon your fields
and until we meet again,
may God hold you in the palm of his hand.

Traditional

YOUTHWORK MAGAZINE

Martin Saunders is the Editor of *Youthwork* magazine, the UK's most popular youth ministry resource. Every month, *Youthwork* is packed with resources, ideas and inspiration to help you in your work with young people. Each issue of *Youthwork* includes:

- an adaptable discussion starter
- four session plans, rooted in the Bible and tackling key themes for young people
- movie clips from the latest DVDs, applied for your work with youth
- drama sketches, designed for use in a range of contexts
- in-depth updates on developments in youth culture
- longer articles by the world's leading youth work writers
- reviews of the latest resources
- stories from on the ground youth workers
- plus news, interviews, regular columns and more!

To subscribe now, and receive a great free gift, visit www.youthwork.co.uk/subscribe

The Think Tank
by Martin Saunders

This book contains 100 FREE TO PHOTOCOPY stories designed to provoke discussion, followed by penetrating questions which relate the stories to biblical bedrock.
The stories are in four parts:

- **WOULD YOU BELIEVE IT?**
  – Unbelievable stories, all absolutely true!

- **INSPIRING INDIVIDUALS** –
  Stories of celebrities, public figures and other people of note making a positive difference.

- **WHAT WOULD YOU DO?** – Ethics explored through stories, many based on real events.

- **TALKING MOVIES** – A major bonus: 25 movie clips that pack a punch with young people, and all the background and questions you'll need to facilitate discussion around them.

Martin Saunders is editor of *Youthwork* magazine, Europe's leading youth ministry magazine resource. He lives to the south of London with his wife Jo and their children.

The book is produced in large clear print and strongly bound for durability.
Includes licence to photocopy

ISBN 978-1-85424-964-7 £12.99 UK / $15.99 US

www.lionhudson.com/monarch

MONARCH

The Ideas Factory
by Martin Saunders

"The hard work of preparing another youth group session just got easier, and – more importantly – the impact of that effort will go deeper."

Russell Rook, Director, ALOVE

The Ideas Factory is a priceless resource for youth leaders.

The 100 spreads contain a story on the left-hand page, matched by questions on the right. Each explores a topic pertinent to young people, such as drugs, truancy, or parental relationships; or an important biblical concept, such as giving, the afterlife, or love. The questions begin with general issues, before moving on to what the Bible has to say.

The last 25 discussion starters provide a journey through the main stories and themes of the Bible.

Martin Saunders is editor of *Youthwork* magazine, Europe's leading youth ministry magazine resource. He lives to the south of London with his wife Jo and their children.

The book is produced in large clear print and strongly bound for durability.

Includes licence to photocopy

ISBN 978-1-85424-834-3 £11.99 UK
ISBN 978-0-8254-6173-6 $14.99 US

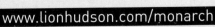
www.lionhudson.com/monarch

MONARCH

Stories From the Edge
by Dave Wiles

A practical resource for youth workers

These true stories are instructive, inspiring, arresting and shocking.

• Meet the 16-year-old on probation, who is on suicide watch

• Mediate between a rebellious youngster and his too-strict dad

• Listen to a 21-year-old girl, with two children in care, who works the street to pay for the heroin her father deals.

Each chapter follows a particular theme, such as "Dads and Lads" or "Youth Culture and Gangs", and ends with points for discussion.

Dave Wiles is Chief Executive of *Frontier Youth Trust*.

ISBN 978-1-85424-963-0 £10.99 UK

www.lionhudson.com/monarch

MONARCH